JOHN F. KENNEDY

WORD FOR WORD

MAUREEN HARRISON
STEVE GILBERT
EDITORS

EXCELLENT BOOKS
LA JOLLA, CALIFORNIA

EXCELLENT BOOKS
Post Office Box 927105
La Jolla, CA 92192-7105

Publisher's Cataloging in Publication Data

John F. Kennedy: Word for Word/
 Maureen Harrison, Steve Gilbert, editors.
 p. cm. - (Word for Word Series)
Bibliography:p.
Includes Index.
1. Kennedy, John F., 1917-1963. 2. United States - Presidents.
I. Title. II. Harrison, Maureen. III. Gilbert, Steve.
IV. Series: Word for Word.
E838.5 K.42 1993   LC 93-072416
973.92-dc20
ISBN 1-880780-03-8

Introduction

I, John Fitzgerald Kennedy, do solemnly swear that I will faithfully execute the Office of President of the United States, and will to the best of my ability, preserve, protect and defend the Constitution of the United States. So help me God.

John F. Kennedy was inaugurated the thirty-fifth President of the United States on January 20, 1961. His Presidency lasted slightly more than a thousand days. Thirty years after his death we have taken this opportunity to look back, not on what historians or biographers have had to say about his life and times but what he had to say about himself.

John F. Kennedy: Word For Word, a selection of the speeches and writings of John Kennedy, is our attempt to paint, using his own words as our brushstrokes, a portrait of the man and America in the early Sixties. We have selected from the Kennedy candidacy and the Kennedy Presidency, a period of three years, documents on the most important issues of the day: the threat of nuclear war, the emerging civil rights movement, the embryonic women's rights movement, and the dangerous Cold War confrontations over Cuba, Berlin, and Southeast Asia.

We have included in *John F. Kennedy: Word For Word* thirty separate documents which, read individually, give a partial picture of the times, and, read as a whole, reveal a full-length portrait of the man behind the words. Theodore Roosevelt called the American Presidency "A Bully Pulpit." John F. Kennedy used the pulpit of the Presidency to preach sacrifice, perseverance, courage, tolerance, commitment, strength, flexibility, and patience.

Unlike their predecessors, modern presidents do not now, and did not in the Kennedy era, write, word for word, their own speeches. Thomas Jefferson, writing the Declaration of Independence by candlelight, or Abraham Lincoln, writing the Gettysburg Address on the back of an envelope, are anachronisms in the modern world. But the Kennedy speechwriters, chief among them Theodore Sorensen, Richard Goodwin, and Arthur Schlesinger, Jr., did not put words into the mouth of a talking head. The Kennedy speechwriters were not so much ghosts as kindred spirits; they understood what their President wanted to say and, when John F. Kennedy read their prepared texts, he spoke for himself. We believe the speeches and writings selected for this book represent the essential beliefs, political philosophy, and moral outlook of John F. Kennedy.

The editors offer their thanks to the reference librarians of Harvard University; the John F. Kennedy Presidential Library, in Cambridge, Massachusetts; the New York Public Library; Columbia University; and especially of the Library of Congress, in Washington, DC.

The life and death of John F. Kennedy have been extensively chronicled in books of varying quality and accuracy throughout the years. We have included in our bibliography what we consider the best of the Kennedy biographies and histories.

The voice of John F. Kennedy was stilled in Dallas on November 22, 1963. We hope that this book will serve to keep an echo of his voice alive.

M.H. & S.G.

This book is dedicated to Cliff Pattick who,
like all his generation,
knows exactly where he was on
November 22, 1963

*A man does what he must - in spite of personal
consequences, in spite of obstacles and dangers and
pressures - and that is the basis of all human morality.*
John F. Kennedy, **Profiles In Courage**

Table of Contents

The Bay of Pigs
51

While refraining from military intervention in Cuba, the people of the United States do not conceal their admiration for Cuban patriots who wish to see a democratic system in an independent Cuba.

The President and the Press
53

An error doesn't become a mistake until you refuse to correct it. We intend to accept full responsibility for our errors; and we expect you to point them out when we miss them.

Europe
63

We must be patient. We must be determined. We must be courageous. We must accept both risks and burdens, but with the will and the work freedom will prevail.

Annapolis
75

The answer to those who challenge us so severely in so many parts of the globe lies in our willingness to freely commit ourselves to the maintenance of our country and the things for which it stands.

The Berlin Crisis
81

We have given our word that an attack upon that city will be regarded as an attack upon us all.

Presidential Inability
97
Unlike the case of removal, death, or resignation, the Vice President does not permanently become the President.

1961 United Nations Address
101
Never have the nations of the world had so much to lose, or so much to gain. Together we shall save our planet, or together we shall perish in its flames.

Women
119
Women have basic rights which should be respected and fostered as part of our Nation's commitment to human dignity, freedom, and democracy.

1962 State of the Union Address
125
Our basic goal remains the same: a peaceful world community of free and independent states - free to choose their own future and their own system, so long as it does not threaten the freedom of others.

Nuclear Testing
151
I am sworn to uphold and defend the freedom of the American people - and I intend to do whatever must be done to fulfill that solemn obligation.

Berkeley
165
Knowledge transcends national antagonisms - it speaks a universal language - it is the possession, not of a single class, or of a single nation or a single ideology, but of all mankind.

Nobel Prize Winners
173
I think this is the most extraordinary collection of talent, of human knowledge, that has ever been gathered together at the White House, with the possible exception of when Thomas Jefferson dined alone.

West Point
177
We go forth confident of support and success because we know that we are working and fighting for each other and for all those men and women all over the globe who are determined to be free.

Yale
185
The great enemy of truth is very often not the lie - deliberate, contrived, and dishonest - but the myth - persistent, persuasive, and unrealistic.

Independence Hall
199
Others may confine themselves to debate, discussion, and that ultimate luxury - free advice. Our responsibility is one of decision - for to govern is to choose.

Civil Rights
247

Americans are free to disagree with the law but not to disobey it. In a government of laws and not of men, no man, however prominent or powerful, and no mob, however unruly or boisterous, is entitled to defy a court of law.

Air Force Academy
269

For an imperfect world where human folly has been the rule and not the exception, the surest way to bring on the war that can never happen is to sit back and assure ourselves it will never happen.

Ich Bin Ein Berliner
277

All free men, wherever they may live, are citizens of Berlin, and, therefore, as a free man, I take pride in the words, "Ich bin ein Berliner."

Physical Fitness
281

The fitness of our people is one of the foundation stones of our national greatness.

1963 United Nations Address
289

Peace is a daily, a weekly, a monthly process, gradually changing opinions, slowly eroding old barriers, quietly building new structures. And however undramatic the pursuit of peace, that pursuit must go on.

The Ungiven Speech
303

We in this country, in this generation, are - by destiny rather than choice - the watchmen on the walls of world freedom.

Acceptance Speech
Democratic National Convention
Los Angeles, California
July 15, 1960

With a deep sense of duty and high resolve, I accept your nomination. I accept it with a full and grateful heart - without reservation - and with only one obligation - the obligation to devote every effort of body, mind and spirit to lead our party back to victory and our nation back to greatness.

I am grateful, too, that you have provided me with such an eloquent statement of our party's platform. Pledges which are made so eloquently are made to be kept. "The rights of man" - the civil and economic rights essential to the human dignity of all men - are indeed our goal and our first principles. This is a platform on which I can run with enthusiasm and conviction.

And I am grateful, finally, that I can rely in the coming months on so many others - on a distinguished running-mate who brings unity to our ticket and strength to our platform, Lyndon Johnson - on one of the most articulate statesmen of our time, Adlai Stevenson - on a great spokesman for our needs as a nation and a people, Stuart Symington - and on that fighting campaigner whose support I welcome, President Harry S. Truman.

I feel a lot safer now that they are on my side again. And I am proud of the contrast with our Republican competitors. For their ranks are apparently so thin that not one challenger has come forth with both the competence and the courage to make theirs an open convention.

I am fully aware of the fact that the Democratic party, by nominating someone of my faith, has taken on what many regard as a new and hazardous risk - new, at least, since 1928. But I look at it this way:

The Democratic Party has once again placed its confidence in the American people, and in their ability to render a free, fair judgment.

And you have, at the same time, placed your confidence in me, and in my ability to render a free, fair judgment - to uphold the Constitution and my oath of office - and to reject any kind of religious pressure or obligation that might directly or indirectly interfere with my conduct of the Presidency in the national interest.

My record of fourteen years supporting public education - supporting complete separation of church and state - and resisting pressures from any source on any issue should be clear by now to everyone.

I hope that no American, considering the really critical issues facing this country, will waste his franchise by voting either for me or against me solely on account of my religious affiliation. It is not relevant, I want to stress, what some other political or religious leader may have said on this subject. It is not relevant what abuses may have existed in other countries or in other times. It is not relevant what pressures, if any, might conceivably be brought to bear on me.

I am telling you now what you are entitled to know:

That my decisions on every public policy will be my own - as an American, a Democrat and a free man.

Under any circumstances, however, the victory we seek in November will not be easy. We all know that in our hearts. We recognize the power of the forces that will be aligned against us. We know they will invoke the name of Abraham Lincoln on behalf of their candidate - despite the fact that his political career has often seemed to show charity toward none and malice for all.

We know that it will not be easy to campaign against a man who has spoken or voted on every known side of every known issue. Mr. Nixon may feel it is his turn now, after the New Deal and the Fair Deal - but before he deals, someone had better cut the cards.

That "someone" may be the millions of Americans who voted for President Eisenhower but balk at his would-be, self-appointed successor. For just as historians tell us that Richard I was not fit to fill the shoes of bold Henry II - and that Richard Cromwell was not fit to wear the mantle of his uncle - they might add in future years that Richard Nixon did not measure to the footsteps of Dwight D. Eisenhower.

Perhaps he could carry on the party policies - the policies of Nixon, Benson, Dirksen and Goldwater. But this nation cannot afford such a luxury. Perhaps we could afford a Coolidge following Harding. And perhaps we could afford a Pierce following Fillmore.

But after Buchanan this nation needed a Lincoln - after Taft, we needed a Wilson - after Hoover we needed Franklin Roosevelt - and after eight years of drugged and fitful sleep, this nation needs strong, creative Democratic leadership in the White House.

But we are not merely running against Mr. Nixon. Our task is not merely one of itemizing Republican failures. Nor is that wholly necessary. For the families forced from the farm will know how to vote without our telling them. The unemployed miners and textile workers will know how to vote. The old people without medical care - the families without a decent home - the parents of children without adequate food or schools - they all know that it's time for a change. But I think the American people expect more from us than cries of indignation and attack. The times are too grave, the challenge too urgent, and the stakes too high - to permit the customary passions of political debate. We are not here to curse the darkness, but to light the candle that can guide us through that darkness to a safe and sane future. As Winston Churchill said on taking office some twenty years ago:

"If we open a quarrel between the present and the past, we shall be in danger of losing the future."

Today our concern must be with that future. For the world is changing. The old era is ending. The old ways will not do.

Abroad, the balance of power is shifting. There are new and more terrible weapons - new and uncertain nations - new pressures of population and deprivation. One-third of the world, it has been said, may be free - but one-third is the victim of cruel repression - and the other one-third is rocked by the pangs of poverty, hunger and envy. More energy is released by the awakening of these new nations than by the fission of the atom itself.

Meanwhile, Communist influence has penetrated further into Asia, stood astride the Middle East and now festers some ninety miles off the coast of Florida. Friends have slipped into neutrality - and neutrals into hostility. As our keynoter reminded us, the President who began his career by going to Korea ends it by staying away from Japan.

The world has been close to war before - but now man, who has survived all previous threats to his existence, has taken into his mortal hands the power to exterminate the entire species some seven times over.

Here at home, the changing fact of the future is equally revolutionary. The New Deal and the Fair Deal were bold measures for their generations - but this is a new generation.

A technological revolution on the farm has led to an output explosion - but we have not yet learned to harness that explosion usefully, while protecting our farmers' right to full parity income.

An urban population revolution has overcrowded our schools, cluttered up our suburbs, and increased the squalor of our slums.

A peaceful revolution for human rights - demanding an end to racial discrimination in all parts of our community life - has strained at the leashes imposed by timid Executive leadership.

A medical revolution has extended the life of our elder citizens without providing the dignity and security those later years deserve. And a revolution of automation finds machines replacing men in the mines and mills of America, without replacing their income or their training or their need to pay the family doctor, grocer and landlord.

There has also been a change - a slippage - in our intellectual and moral strength. Seven lean years of drought and famine have withered the field of ideas. Blight has descended on our regulatory agencies - and a dry rot, beginning in Washington, is seeping into every corner of America - in the payola mentality, the expense account way of life, the confusion between what is legal and what is right. Too many Americans have lost their way, their will and their sense of historic purpose.

It is time, in short, for a new generation of leadership - new men to cope with new problems and new opportunities.

All over the world, particularly in the newer nations, young men are coming to power - men who are not bound by the traditions of the past - men who are not blinded by the old fears and hates and rivalries - young men who can cast off the old slogans and delusions and suspicions.

The Republican nominee-to-be, of course is also a young man. But his approach is as old as McKinley. His party is the party of the past. His speeches are generalities from Poor Richard's Almanac. Their platform, made up of leftover Democratic planks, has the courage of our old convictions. Their pledge is a pledge to the status quo - and today there can be no status quo.

For I stand tonight facing west on what was once the last frontier. From the lands that stretch 3,000 miles behind me, the pioneers of old gave up their safety, their comfort and sometimes their lives to build a new world here in the West.

They were not the captives of their own doubts, the prisoners of their own price tags. Their motto was not "every man for himself" - but "all for the common cause." They were determined to make that new world strong and free, to overcome its hazards and its hardships, to conquer the enemies that threatened from without and within.

Today some would say that those struggles are all over - that all the horizons have been explored - that all the battles have been won - that there is no longer an American frontier.

But I trust that no one in this vast assemblage will agree with those sentiments. For the problems are not all solved and the battles are not all won - and we stand today on the edge of a new frontier - the frontier of the 1960's - a frontier of unknown opportunities and perils - a frontier of unfulfilled hopes and threats.

Woodrow Wilson's New Freedom promised our nation a new political and economic framework. Franklin Roosevelt's New Deal promised security and succor to those in need. But the New Frontier of which I speak is not a set of promises - it is a set of challenges. It sums up not what I intend to offer the American people, but what I intend to ask of them. It appeals to their pride, not their pocketbook - it holds out the promise of more sacrifice instead of more security.

But I tell you the New Frontier is here, whether we seek it or not. Beyond that frontier are uncharted areas of science and space, unsolved problems of peace and war, unconquered pockets of ignorance and prejudice, unanswered questions of poverty and surplus.

It would be easier to shrink back from that frontier, to look to the safe mediocrity of the past, to be lulled by good intentions and high rhetoric - and those who prefer that course should not cast their votes for me, regardless of party.

But I believe the times demand invention, innovation, imagination, decision. I am asking each of you to be new pioneers on that New Frontier. My call is to the young in heart, regardless of age - to the stout in spirit, regardless of party - to all who respond to the scriptural call:

"Be strong and of good courage; be not afraid, neither be thou dismayed."

For courage - not complacency - is our need today - leadership - not salesmanship. And the only valid test of leadership is the ability to lead, and lead vigorously. A tired nation, said David Lloyd George, is a tory nation - and the United States today cannot afford to be either tired or tory.

There may be those who wish to hear more - more promises to this group or that more harsh rhetoric about the men in the Kremlin - more assurances of a golden future, where taxes are always low and subsidies ever high. But my promises are in the platform you have adopted. Our ends will not be won by rhetoric and we can have faith in the future only if we have faith in ourselves.

For the harsh facts of the matter are that we stand on this frontier at a turning-point in history. We must prove all over again whether this nation - or any nation so conceived - can long endure - whether our society - with its freedom of choice, its breadth of opportunity, its range of alternatives - can compete with the single-minded advance of the Communist system.

Can a nation organized and governed such as ours endure? That is the real question. Have we the nerve and the will? Can we carry through in an age where we will witness not only new breakthroughs in weapons of destruction - but also a race for mastery of the sky and the rain, the ocean and the tides, the far side of space and the inside of men's minds?

Are we up to the task? Are we equal to the challenge? Are we willing to match the Russian sacrifice of the present for the future? Or must we sacrifice our future in order to enjoy the present?

That is the question of the New Frontier. That is the choice our nation must make - a choice that lies not merely between two men or two parties, but between the public interest and private comfort - between national greatness and national decline - between the fresh air of progress and the stale, dank atmosphere of "normalcy" - between determined dedication and creeping mediocrity.

All mankind waits upon our decision. A whole world looks to see what we will do. We cannot fail their trust; we cannot fail to try.

It has been a long road from that first snowy day in New Hampshire to this crowded convention city. Now begins another long journey, taking me into your cities and homes all over America. Give me your help, your hand, your voice, your vote. Recall with me the words of Isaiah:

"They that wait upon the Lord shall renew their strength; they shall mount up with wings as eagles; they shall run, and not be weary."

As we face the coming challenge, we too, shall wait upon the Lord and ask that He renew our strength. Then shall we be equal to the test. Then we shall not be weary. And then we shall prevail.

Opening Statement
First Kennedy - Nixon Debate
Chicago, Illinois
September 26, 1960

In the election of 1860, Abraham Lincoln said the question was whether this nation could exist half-slave or half-free. In the election of 1960, and with the world around us, the question is whether the world will exist half-slave or half-free, whether it will move in the direction of freedom, in the direction of the road that we are taking, or whether it will move in the direction of slavery. I think it will depend in great measure upon what we do here in the United States, on the kind of society that we build, on the kind of strength that we maintain.

We discuss tonight domestic issues, but I would not want any implication to be given that this does not involve directly our struggle with Mr. Khrushchev for survival. Mr. Khrushchev is in New York, and he maintains the Communist offensive throughout the world because of the productive power of the Soviet Union itself. The Chinese Communists have always had a large population. But they are important and dangerous now because they are mounting a major effort within their own country. The kind of country we have here, the kind of society we have, the kind of strength we build in the United States will be the defense of freedom. If we do well here, if we meet our obligations, if we're moving ahead, then I think freedom will be secure around the world. If we fail, then freedom fails.

Therefore, I think the question before the American people is: Are we doing as much as we can do? Are we as strong as we should be? Are we as strong as we must be if we're going to maintain our independence, and if we're going to maintain and hold out the hand of friendship to those who look to us for assistance, to those who look to us for survival? I should make it very clear that I do not think we're doing enough, that I am not satisfied as an American with the progress that we're making. This is a great country, but I think it could be a greater country; and this is a powerful country, but I think it could be a more powerful country. I'm not satisfied to have fifty per cent of our steel-mill capacity unused. I'm not satisfied when the United States had last year the lowest rate of economic growth of any major industrialized society in the world. Because economic growth means strength and vitality; it means we're able to sustain our defenses; it means we're able to meet our commitments abroad. I'm not satisfied when we have over nine billion dollars worth of food - some of it rotting - even though there is a hungry world, and even though four million Americans wait every month for a food package from the government, which averages five cents a day per individual. I saw cases in West Virginia, here in the United States, where children took home part of their school lunch in order to feed their families.

I don't think we're meeting our obligations toward these Americans. I'm not satisfied when the Soviet Union is turning out twice as many scientists and engineers as we are. I'm not satisfied when many of our teachers are inadequately paid, or when our children go to school part-time shifts. I think we should have an educational system second to none. I'm not satisfied when I see men like Jimmy Hoffa - in charge of the largest union in the United States - still free. I'm not satisfied when we are failing to develop the natural resources of the United

States to the fullest. Here in the United States, which developed the Tennessee Valley and which built the Grand Coulee and the other dams in the Northwest United States. At the present rate of hydropower production - and that is the hallmark of an industrialized society - the Soviet Union by 1975 will be producing more power than we are. These are all the things, I think, in this country that can make our society strong, or can mean that it stands still.

I'm not satisfied until every American enjoys his full constitutional rights. If a Negro baby is born - and this is true also of Puerto Ricans and Mexicans in some of our cities - he has about one-half as much chance to get through high school as a white baby. He has one-third as much chance to get through college as a white student. He has about a third as much chance to be a professional man, about half as much chance to own a house. He has about four times as much chance that he'll be out of work in his life as the white baby. I think we can do better. I don't want the talents of any American to go to waste.

I know that there are those who say that we want to turn everything over to the government. I don't at all. I want the individuals to meet their responsibilities. And I want the states to meet their responsibilities. But I think there is also a national responsibility. The argument has been used against every piece of social legislation in the last twenty-five years.

The people of the United States individually could not have developed the Tennessee Valley; collectively they could have. A cotton farmer in Georgia or a peanut farmer or a dairy farmer in Wisconsin and Minnesota, he cannot protect himself against the forces of supply and demand in the market place; but working together in effective governmental programs he can do so.

Seventeen million Americans, who live over sixty-five on an average Social Security check of about seventy-eight dollars a month, they're not able to sustain themselves individually, but they can sustain themselves through the social security system. I don't believe in big government, but I believe in effective governmental action. And I think that's the only way that the United States is going to maintain its freedom. It's the only way that we're going to move ahead. I think we can do a better job. I think we're going to have to do a better job if we are going to meet the responsibilities which time and events have placed upon us. We cannot turn the job over to anyone else.

If the United States fails, then the whole cause of freedom fails. And I think it depends in great measure on what we do here in this country. The reason Franklin Roosevelt was a good neighbor in Latin America was because he was a good neighbor in the United States. Because they felt that the American society was moving again. I want us to recapture that image. I want people in Latin America and Africa and Asia to start to look to America; to see how we're doing things; to wonder what the President of the United States is doing; and not to look at Khrushchev, or look at the Chinese Communists. That is the obligation upon our generation.

In 1933, Franklin Roosevelt said in his inaugural that this generation of Americans has a rendezvous with destiny. I think our generation of Americans has the same rendezvous. The question now is: Can freedom be maintained under the most severe attack it has ever

known? I think it can be. And I think in the final
analysis it depends upon what we do here. I think it's
time America started moving again.

Inaugural Address
Washington, DC
January 20, 1961

We observe today not a victory of party but a celebration of freedom - symbolizing an end as well as a beginning - signifying renewal as well as change. For I have sworn before you and Almighty God the same solemn oath our forebears prescribed nearly a century and three quarters ago.

The world is very different now. For man holds in his mortal hands the power to abolish all forms of human poverty and all forms of human life. And yet the same revolutionary beliefs for which our forebears fought are still at issue around the globe - the belief that the rights of man come not from the generosity of the state but from the hand of God.

We dare not forget today that we are the heirs of that first revolution. Let the word go forth from this time and place, to friend and foe alike, that the torch has been passed to a new generation of Americans - born in this century, tempered by war, disciplined by a hard and bitter peace, proud of our ancient heritage - and unwilling to witness or permit the slow undoing of those human rights to which this nation has always been committed, and to which we are committed today at home and around the world.

Let every nation know, whether it wishes us well or ill, that we shall pay any price, bear any burden, meet any hardship, support any friend, oppose any foe to assure the survival and the success of liberty.

This much we pledge - and more.

To those old allies whose cultural and spiritual origins we share, we pledge the loyalty of faithful friends. United, there is little we cannot do in a host of cooperative ventures. Divided, there is little we can do for we dare not meet a powerful challenge at odds and split asunder.

To those new states whom we welcome to the ranks of the free, we pledge our word that one form of colonial control shall not have passed away merely to be replaced by a far more iron tyranny. We shall not always expect to find them supporting our view. But we shall always hope to find them strongly supporting their own freedom - and to remember that, in the past, those who foolishly sought power by riding the back of the tiger ended up inside.

To those peoples in the huts and villages of half the globe struggling to break the bonds of mass misery, we pledge our best efforts to help them help themselves, for whatever period is required - not because the communists may be doing it, not because we seek their votes, but because it is right. If a free society cannot help the many who are poor, it cannot save the few who are rich.

To our sister republics south of our border, we offer a special pledge - to convert our good words into good deeds - in a new alliance for progress - to assist free men and free governments in casting off the chains of poverty. But this peaceful revolution of hope cannot become the prey of hostile powers. Let all our neighbors know that we shall join with them to oppose aggression or subversion anywhere in the Americas. And let every other power know that this Hemisphere intends to remain the master of its own house.

To that world assembly of sovereign states, the United Nations, our last best hope in an age where the instruments of war have far outpaced the instruments of peace, we renew our pledge of support - to prevent it from becoming merely a forum for invective - to strengthen its shield of the new and the weak - and to enlarge the area in which its writ may run.

Finally, to those nations who would make themselves our adversary, we offer not a pledge but a request: that both sides begin anew the quest for peace, before the dark powers of destruction unleashed by science engulf all humanity in planned or accidental self-destruction.

We dare not tempt them with weakness. For only when our arms are sufficient beyond doubt can we be certain beyond doubt that they will never be employed.

But neither can two great and powerful groups of nations take comfort from our present course - both sides overburdened by the cost of modern weapons, both rightly alarmed by the steady spread of the deadly atom, yet both racing to alter that uncertain balance of terror that stays the hand of mankind's final war.

So let us begin anew - remembering on both sides that civility is not a sign of weakness, and sincerity is always subject to proof. Let us never negotiate out of fear. But let us never fear to negotiate.

Let both sides explore what problems unite us instead of belaboring those problems which divide us.

Let both sides, for the first time, formulate serious and precise proposals for the inspection and control of arms - and bring the absolute power to destroy other nations under the absolute control of all nations.

Let both sides seek to invoke the wonders of science instead of its terrors. Together let us explore the stars, conquer the deserts, eradicate disease, tap the ocean depths and encourage the arts and commerce. Let both sides unite to heed in all corners of the earth the command of Isaiah - to "undo the heavy burdens . . . [and] let the oppressed go free."

And if a beach-head of cooperation may push back the jungle of suspicion, let both sides join in creating a new endeavor, not a new balance of power, but a new world of law, where the strong are just and the weak secure and the peace preserved.

All this will not be finished in the first one hundred days. Nor will it be finished in the first one thousand days, nor in the life of this Administration, nor even perhaps in our lifetime on this planet. But let us begin.

In your hands, my fellow citizens, more than mine, will rest the final success or failure of our course. Since this country was founded, each generation of Americans has been summoned to give testimony to its national loyalty. The graves of young Americans who answered the call to service surround the globe.

Now the trumpet summons us again - not as a call to bear arms, though arms we need - not as a call to battle, though embattled we are - but a call to bear the burden of a long twilight struggle, year in and year out, "rejoicing in hope, patient in tribulation" - a struggle against the common enemies of man: tyranny, poverty, disease and war itself.

Can we forge against these enemies a grand and global alliance, North and South, East and West, that can assure a more fruitful life for all mankind? Will you join in that historic effort?

In the long history of the world, only a few generations have been granted the role of defending freedom in its hour of maximum danger. I do not shrink from this responsibility - I welcome it. I do not believe that any of us would exchange places with any other people or any other generation. The energy, the faith, the devotion which we bring to this endeavor will light our country and all who serve it - and the glow from that fire can truly light the world.

And so, my fellow Americans: ask not what your country can do for you - ask what you can do for your country.

My fellow citizens of the world: ask not what America will do for you, but what together we can do for the freedom of man.

Finally, whether you are citizens of America or citizens of the world, ask of us here the same high standards of strength and sacrifice which we ask of you. With a good conscience our only sure reward, with history the final judge of our deeds, let us go forth to lead the land we love, asking His blessing and His help, but knowing that here on earth God's work must truly be our own.

The State of the Union
Washington, DC
January 30, 1961

It is a pleasure to return from whence I came. You are among my oldest friends in Washington - and this House is my oldest home. It was here, more than 14 years ago, that I first took the oath of Federal office. It was here, for 14 years, that I gained both knowledge and inspiration from members of both parties in both Houses - from your wise and generous leaders - and from the pronouncements which I can vividly recall, sitting where you now sit - including the programs of two great Presidents, the undimmed eloquence of Churchill, the soaring idealism of Nehru, the steadfast words of General de Gaulle. To speak from this same historic rostrum is a sobering experience. To be back among so many friends is a happy one.

I am confident that that friendship will continue. Our Constitution wisely assigns both joint and separate roles to each branch of the government; and a President and a Congress who hold each other in mutual respect will neither permit nor attempt any trespass. For my part, I shall withhold from neither the Congress nor the people any fact or report, past, present or future, which is necessary for an informed judgment of our conduct and hazards. I shall neither shift the burden of executive decisions to the Congress, nor avoid responsibility for the outcome of those decisions.

I speak today in an hour of national peril and national opportunity. Before my term has ended, we shall have to test anew whether a nation organized and governed such as ours can endure. The outcome is by no means certain.

The answers are by no means clear. All of us together - this Administration, this Congress, this nation - must forge those answers.

But today, were I to offer - after little more than a week in office - detailed legislation to remedy every national ill, the Congress would rightly wonder whether the desire for speed had replaced the duty of responsibility.

My remarks, therefore, will be limited. But they will also be candid. To state the facts frankly is not to despair the future nor indict the past. The prudent heir takes careful inventory of his legacies, and gives a faithful accounting to those whom he owes an obligation of trust. And, while the occasion does not call for another recital of our blessings and assets, we do have no greater asset than the willingness of a free and determined people, through its elected officials, to face all problems frankly and meet all dangers free from panic or fear.

The present state of our economy is disturbing. We take office in the wake of seven months of recession, three and one-half years of slack, seven years of diminished economic growth, and nine years of falling farm income.

Business bankruptcies have reached their highest level since the Great Depression. Since 1951 farm income has been squeezed down by 25 percent. Save for a brief period in 1958, insured unemployment is at the highest peak in our history. Of some five and one-half million Americans who are without jobs, more than one million have been searching for work for more than four months. And during each month some 150,000 workers are exhausting their already meager jobless benefit rights.

Nearly one-eighth of those who are without jobs live almost without hope in nearly one hundred especially depressed and troubled areas. The rest include new school graduates unable to use their talents, farmers forced to give up their part-time jobs which helped balance their family budgets, skilled and unskilled workers laid off in such important industries as metals, machinery, automobiles and apparel.

Our recovery from the 1958 recession, moreover, was anemic and incomplete. Our Gross National Product never regained its full potential. Unemployment never returned to normal levels. Maximum use of our national industrial capacity was never restored.

In short, the American economy is in trouble. The most resourceful industrialized country on earth ranks among the last in the rate of economic growth. Since last spring our economic growth rate has actually receded. Business investment is in a decline. Profits have fallen below predicted levels. Construction is off. A million unsold automobiles are in inventory. Fewer people are working - and the average work week has shrunk well below 40 hours. Yet prices have continued to rise - so that now too many Americans have *less* to spend for items that cost *more* to buy.

Economic prophecy is at best an uncertain art - as demonstrated by the prediction one year ago from this same podium that 1960 would be, and I quote, "the most prosperous year in our history." Nevertheless, forecasts of continued slack and only slightly reduced unemployment through 1961 and 1962 have been made with alarming unanimity - and this Administration does not intend to stand helplessly by.

We cannot afford to waste idle hours and empty plants while awaiting the end of the recession. We must show the world what a free economy can do - to reduce unemployment, to put unused capacity to work, to spur new productivity, and to foster higher economic growth within a range of sound fiscal policies and relative price stability.

I will propose to the Congress within the next 14 days measures to improve unemployment compensation through temporary increases in duration on a self-supporting basis - to provide more food for the families of the unemployed, and to aid their needy children - to redevelop our areas of chronic labor surplus - to expand the services of the U.S. Employment Offices to stimulate housing and construction - to secure more purchasing power for our lowest paid workers by raising and expanding the minimum wage - to offer tax incentives for sound plant investment - to increase the development of our natural resources - to encourage price stability - and to take other steps aimed at insuring a prompt recovery and paving the way for increased long-range growth. This is not a partisan program concentrating on our weaknesses - it is, I hope, a national program to realize our national strength.

Efficient expansion at home, stimulating the new plant and technology that can make our goods more competitive, is also the key to the international balance of payments problem. Laying aside all alarmist talk and panicky solutions, let us put that knotty problem in its proper perspective. It is true that, since 1958, the gap between the dollars we spend or invest abroad and the dollars returned to us has substantially widened. This overall deficit in our balance of payments increased by nearly $11 billion in the 3 years - and holders of dollars abroad converted them to gold in such a quantity as to cause a total outflow of nearly $5 billion of gold from our reserve. The 1959 deficit was caused in large part by the failure of our exports to penetrate foreign markets - the result both of restrictions on our goods and our own uncompetitive prices. The 1960 deficit, on the other hand, was more the result of an increase in private capital outflow seeking new opportunity, higher return or speculative advantage abroad.

Meanwhile this country has continued to bear more than its share of the West's military and foreign aid obligations. Under existing policies, another deficit of $2 billion is predicted for 1961 - and individuals in those countries whose dollar position once depended on these deficits for improvement now wonder aloud whether our gold reserves will remain sufficient to meet our own obligations.

All this is cause for concern - but it is not cause for panic. For our monetary and financial position remains exceedingly strong. Including our drawing rights in the International Monetary Fund and the gold reserve held as backing for our currency and Federal Reserve deposits, we have some $22 billion in total gold stocks and other international monetary reserves available - and I now pledge that their full strength stands behind the value of the dollar for use if needed.

Moreover, we hold large assets abroad - the total owed this nation far exceeds the claims upon our reserves - and our exports once again substantially exceed our imports.

In short, we need not - and we shall not - take any action to increase the dollar price of gold from $35 an ounce - to impose exchange controls - to reduce our anti-recession efforts - to fall back on restrictive trade policies - or to weaken our commitments around the world.

This Administration will not distort the value of the dollar in any fashion. And this is a commitment.

Prudence and good sense do require, however, that new steps betaken to ease the payments deficit and prevent any gold crisis. Our success in world affairs has long depended in part upon foreign confidence in our ability to pay. A series of executive orders, legislative remedies and cooperative efforts with our allies will get underway immediately - aimed at attracting foreign investment and travel to this country - promoting American exports, at stable prices and with more liberal government guarantees and financing - curbing tax and customs loopholes that encourage undue spending of private dollars abroad - and (through OECD, NATO and otherwise) sharing with our allies all efforts to provide for the common defense of the free world and the hopes for growth of the less developed lands. While the current deficit lasts, ways will be found to ease our dollar outlays abroad without placing the full burden on the families of men whom we have asked to serve our Flag overseas.

In short, whatever is required will be done to back up all our efforts abroad, and to make certain that, in the future as in the past, the dollar is as "sound as a dollar."

But more than our exchange of international payments is out of balance. The current Federal budget for fiscal

1961 is almost certain to show a net deficit. The budget already submitted for fiscal 1962 will remain in balance only if the Congress enacts all the revenue measures requested - and only if an earlier and sharper upturn in the economy than my economic advisers now think likely produces the tax revenues estimated. Nevertheless, a new Administration must of necessity build on the spending and revenue estimates already submitted. Within that framework, barring the development of urgent national defense needs or a worsening of the economy, it is my current intention to advocate a program of expenditures which, including revenues from a stimulation of the economy, will not of and by themselves unbalance the earlier Budget.

However, we will do what must be done. For our national household is cluttered with unfinished and neglected tasks. Our cities are being engulfed in squalor. Twelve long years after Congress declared our goal to be "a decent home and a suitable environment for every American family," we still have 25 million Americans living in substandard homes. A new housing program under a new Housing and Urban Affairs Department will be needed this year.

Our classrooms contain 2 million more children than they can properly have room for, taught by 90,000 teachers not properly qualified to teach. One third of our most promising high school graduates are financially unable to continue the development of their talents. The war babies of the 1940's, who overcrowded our schools in the 1950's, are now descending in 1960 upon our colleges - with two college students for every one, ten years from now - and our colleges are ill prepared. We lack the scientists, the engineers and the teachers our world obligations require.

We have neglected oceanography, saline water conversion, and the basic research that lies at the root of all progress. Federal grants for both higher and public school education can no longer be delayed.

Medical research has achieved new wonders - but these wonders are too often beyond the reach of too many people, owing to a lack of income (particularly among the aged), a lack of hospital beds, a lack of nursing homes and a lack of doctors and dentists. Measures to provide health care for the aged under Social Security, and to increase the supply of both facilities and personnel, must be undertaken this year.

Our supply of clean water is dwindling. Organized and juvenile crimes cost the taxpayers millions of dollars each year, making it essential that we have improved enforcement and new legislative safeguards. The denial of constitutional rights to some of our fellow Americans on account of race - at the ballot box and elsewhere - disturbs the national conscience, and subjects us to the charge of world opinion that our democracy is not equal to the high promise of our heritage. Morality in private business has not been sufficiently spurred by morality in public business. A host of problems and projects in all 50 States, though not possible to include in this Message, deserves - and will receive - the attention of both the Congress and the Executive Branch. On most of these matters, Messages will be sent to the Congress within the next two weeks.

But all these problems pale when placed beside those which confront us around the world. No man entering upon this office, regardless of his party, regardless of his previous service in Washington, could fail to be staggered upon learning - even in this brief 10 day period - the harsh enormity of the trails through which we must pass in the next four years. Each day the crises multiply. Each day their solution grows more difficult. Each day we draw nearer the hour of maximum danger, as weapons spread and hostile forces grow stronger. I feel I must inform the Congress that our analyses over the last ten days make it clear that - in each of the principal areas of crisis - the tide of events has been running out and time has not been our friend.

In Asia, the relentless pressures of the Chinese Communists menace the security of the entire area - from the borders of India and South Viet Nam to the jungles of Laos, struggling to protect its newly- won independence. We seek in Laos what we seek in all Asia, and, indeed, in all of the world - freedom for the people and independence for the government. And this Nation shall persevere in our pursuit of these objectives.

In Africa, the Congo has been brutally torn by civil strife, political unrest and public disorder. We shall continue to support the heroic efforts of the United Nations to restore peace and order - efforts which are now endangered by mounting tensions, unsolved problems, and decreasing support from many member states.

In Latin America, Communist agents seeking to exploit that region's peaceful revolution of hope have established a base on Cuba, only 90 miles from our shores. Our objection with Cuba is not over the people's drive for a better life. Our objection is to their domination by foreign and domestic tyrannies. Cuban social and economic reform should be encouraged. Questions of economic and trade policy can always be negotiated. But Communist domination in this Hemisphere can never be negotiated.

We are pledged to work with our sister republics to free the Americas of all such foreign domination and all tyranny, working toward the goal of a free hemisphere of free governments, extending from Cape Horn to the Arctic Circle.

In Europe our alliances are unfulfilled and in some disarray. The unity of NATO has been weakened by economic rivalry and partially eroded by national interest. It has not yet fully mobilized its resources nor fully achieved a common outlook. Yet no Atlantic power can meet on its own the mutual problems now facing us in defense, foreign aid, monetary reserves, and a host of other areas; and our close ties with those whose hopes and interests we share are among this Nation's most powerful assets.

Our greatest challenge is still the world that lies beyond the Cold War - but the first great obstacle is still our relations with the Soviet Union and Communist China. We must never be lulled into believing that either power has yielded its ambitions for world domination - ambitions which they forcefully restated only a short time ago. On the contrary, our task is to convince them that aggression and subversion will not be profitable routes to pursue these ends. Open and peaceful competition - for prestige, for markets, for scientific achievement, even for men's minds - is something else again. For if Freedom and Communism were to compete for man's allegiance in a world at peace, I would look to the future with ever increasing confidence.

To meet this array of challenges - to fulfill the role we cannot avoid on the world scene - we must reexamine and revise our whole arsenal of tools: military, economic and political.

One must not overshadow the other. On the Presidential Coat of Arms, the American eagle holds in his right talon the olive branch, while in his left he holds a bundle of arrows. We intend to give equal attention to both.

First, we must strengthen our military tools. We are moving into a period of uncertain risk and great commitment in which both the military and diplomatic possibilities require a Free World force so powerful as to make any aggression clearly futile. Yet in the past, lack of a consistent, coherent military strategy, the absence of basic assumptions about our national requirements and the faulty estimates and duplication arising from inter-service rivalries have all made it difficult to assess accurately how adequate - or inadequate - our defenses really are.

I have, therefore, instructed the Secretary of Defense to reappraise our entire defense strategy - our ability to fulfill our commitments - the effectiveness, vulnerability, and dispersal of our strategic bases, forces and warning systems - the efficiency and economy of our operation and organization - the elimination of obsolete bases and installations - and the adequacy, modernization and mobility of our present conventional and nuclear forces and weapons systems in the light of present and future dangers. I have asked for preliminary conclusions by the end of February - and I then shall recommend whatever legislative, budgetary or executive action is needed in the light of these conclusions.

In the meantime, I have asked the Defense Secretary to initiate immediately three new steps most clearly needed now:

First, I have directed prompt attention to increase our airlift capacity. Obtaining additional air transport mobility - and obtaining it now - will better assure the ability of our conventional forces to respond, with discrimination and speed, to any problem at any spot on the globe at any moment's notice. In particular it will enable us to meet any deliberate effort to avoid or divert our forces by starting limited wars in widely scattered parts of the globe.

I have directed prompt action to step up our Polaris submarine program. Using unobligated shipbuilding funds now (to let contracts originally scheduled for the next fiscal year) will build and place on station - at least nine months earlier than planned - substantially more units of a crucial deterrent - a fleet that will never attack first, but possess sufficient powers of retaliation, concealed beneath the seas, to discourage any aggressor from launching an attack upon our security.

I have directed prompt action to accelerate our entire missile program. Until the Secretary of Defense's reappraisal is completed, the emphasis here will be largely on improved organization and decision-making - on cutting down the wasteful duplications and the time lag that have handicapped our whole family of missiles. If we are to keep the peace, we need an invulnerable missile force powerful enough to deter any aggressor from even threatening an attack that he would know could not destroy enough of our force to prevent his own destruction. For as I said upon taking the oath of office:

"Only when our arms are sufficient beyond doubt can we be certain beyond doubt that they will never be employed."

Secondly, we must improve our economic tools. Our role is essential and unavoidable in the construction of a sound and expanding economy for the entire noncommunist world, helping other nations build the strength to meet their own problems, to satisfy their own aspirations - to surmount their own dangers. The problems in achieving this goal are towering and unprecedented - the response must be towering and unprecedented as well, much as Lend Lease and the Marshall Plan were in earlier years, which brought such fruitful results.

I intend to ask the Congress for authority to establish a new and more effective program for assisting the economic, educational and social development of other countries and continents. That program must stimulate and take more effectively into account the contributions of our allies, and provide central policy direction for all our own programs that now so often overlap, conflict or diffuse our energies and resources. Such a program, compared to past programs, will require: more flexibility for short run emergencies; more commitment to long term development; new attention to education at all levels; greater emphasis on the recipient nation's role, their effort, their purpose, with greater social justice for their people, broader distribution and participation by their people and more efficient public administration and more efficient tax systems of their own; and orderly planning for national and regional development instead of a piecemeal approach.

I hope the Senate will take early action approving the Convention establishing the Organization for Economic Cooperation and Development. This will be an important instrument in sharing with our allies this development effort - working toward the time when each nation will contribute in proportion to its ability to pay. For, while we are prepared to assume our full share of these huge burdens, we cannot and must not be expected to bear them alone.

To our sister republics to the south, we have pledged a new alliance for progress - alianza para progreso. Our goal is a free and prosperous Latin America, realizing for all its states and all its citizens a degree of economic and social progress that matches their historic contributions of culture, intellect and liberty. To start this nation's role at this time in that alliance of neighbors, I am recommending the following:

That the Congress appropriate in full the $500 million fund pledged by the Act of Bogota, to be used not as an instrument of the Cold War, but as a first step in the sound development of the Americas.

That a new Inter-Departmental Task Force be established under the leadership of the Department of State, to coordinate at the highest level all policies and programs of concern to the Americas.

That our delegates to the OAS, working with those of other members, strengthen that body as an instrument to preserve the peace and to prevent foreign domination anywhere in the Hemisphere.

That, in cooperation with other nations, we launch a new hemispheric attack on illiteracy and inadequate educational opportunities to all levels; and finally,

That a Food-for-Peace mission be sent immediately to Latin America to explore ways in which our vast food abundance can be used to help end hunger and malnutrition in certain areas of suffering in our own hemisphere.

This Administration is expanding its Food-for-Peace Program in every possible way. The product of our abundance must be used more effectively to relieve hunger and help economic growth in all corners of the globe. And I have asked the Director of this Program to recommend additional ways in which these surpluses can advance the interest of world peace - including the establishment of world food reserves.

An even more valuable national asset is our reservoir of dedicated men and women - not only on our college campuses but in every age group - who have indicated their desire to contribute their skills, their efforts, and a part of their lives to the fight for world order. We can mobilize this talent through the formation of a National Peace Corps, enlisting the services of all those with the desire and capacity to help foreign lands meet their urgent needs for trained personnel.

Finally, while our attention is centered on the development of the noncommunist world, we must never forget our hopes for the ultimate freedom and welfare of the Eastern European peoples. In order to be prepared to help re-establish historic ties of friendship, I am asking the Congress for increased discretion to use economic tools in this area whenever this is found to be clearly in the national interest. This will require amendment of the Mutual Defense Assistance Control Act along the lines I proposed as a member of the Senate, and upon which the Senate voted last summer. Meanwhile, I hope to explore with the Polish government the possibility of using our frozen Polish funds on projects of peace that will demonstrate our abiding friendship for and interest in the people of Poland.

Third, we must sharpen our political and diplomatic tools - the means of cooperation and agreement on which an enforceable world order must ultimately rest.

I have already taken steps to coordinate and expand our disarmament effort - to increase our programs of research and study - and to make arms control a central goal of our national policy under my direction. The deadly arms race, and the huge resources it absorbs, have too long overshadowed all else we must do. We must prevent that arms race from spreading to new nations, to new nuclear powers and to the reaches of outer space. We must make certain that our negotiators are better informed and better prepared - to formulate workable proposals of our own and to make sound judgments about the proposals of others.

I have asked the other governments concerned to agree to a reasonable delay in the talks on a nuclear test ban - and it is our intention to resume negotiations prepared to reach a final agreement with any nation that is equally willing to agree to an effective and enforceable treaty.

We must increase our support of the United Nations as an instrument to end the Cold War instead of an arena in which to fight it. In recognition of its increasing importance and the doubling of its membership: we are enlarging and strengthening our own mission to the U.N.; we shall help insure that it is properly financed; we shall work to see that the integrity of the office of the Secretary General is maintained; and I would address a special plea to the smaller nations of the world - to join with us in strengthening this organization, which is far more essential to their security than it is to ours - the only body in the world where no nation need be powerful to be secure, where every nation has an equal voice, and where any nation can exert influence not according to the strength of its armies but according to the strength of its ideas. It deserves the support of all.

Finally, this Administration intends to explore promptly all possible areas of cooperation with the Soviet Union and other nations "to invoke the wonders of science instead of its terrors." Specifically, I now invite all nations - including the Soviet Union - to join with us in developing a weather prediction program, in a new communications satellite program and in preparation for probing the distant planets of Mars and Venus, probes which may someday unlock the deepest secrets of the universe.

Today this country is ahead in the science and technology of space, while the Soviet Union is ahead in the capacity to lift large vehicles into orbit. Both nations would help themselves as well as other nations by removing these endeavors from the bitter and wasteful competition of the Cold War.

The United States would be willing to join with the Soviet Union and the scientists of all nations in a greater effort to make the fruits of this new knowledge available to all - and, beyond that, in an effort to extend farm technology to hungry nations - to wipe out disease - to increase the exchanges of scientists and their knowledge - and to make our own laboratories available to technicians of other lands who lack the facilities to pursue their own work. Where nature makes natural allies of us all, we can demonstrate that beneficial relations are possible even with those with whom we most deeply disagree - and this must someday be the basis of world peace and world law.

I have commented on the state of the domestic economy, our balance of payments, our Federal and social budget and the state of the world. I would like to conclude with a few remarks about the state of the Executive branch.

We have found it full of honest and useful public servants - but their capacity to act decisively at the exact time action is needed has too often been muffled in the morass of committees, timidities and fictitious theories which have created a growing gap between decision and execution, between planning and reality. In a time of rapidly deteriorating situations at home and abroad, this is bad for the public service and particularly bad for the country; and we mean to make a change.

I have pledged myself and my colleagues in the cabinet to a continuous encouragement of initiative, responsibility and energy in serving the public interest. Let every public servant know, whether his post is high or low, that a man's rank and reputation in this Administration will be determined by the size of the job he does, and not by the size of his staff, his office or his budget. Let it be clear that this Administration recognizes the value of dissent and daring - that we greet healthy controversy as the hallmark of healthy change. Let the public service be a proud and lively career. And let every man and woman who works in any area of our national government, in any branch, at any level, be able to say with pride and with honor in future years: "I served the United States government in that hour of our nation's need."

For only with complete dedication by us all to the national interest can we bring our country through the troubled years that lie ahead. Our problems are critical. The tide is unfavorable. The news will be worse before it is better. And while hoping and working for the best, we should prepare ourselves now for the worst.

We cannot escape our dangers - neither must we let them drive us into panic or narrow isolation. In many areas of the world where the balance of power already rests with our adversaries, the forces of freedom are sharply divided. It is one of the ironies of our time that the techniques of a harsh and repressive system should be able to instill discipline and ardor in its servants - while the blessings of liberty have too often stood for privilege, materialism and a life of ease.

But I have a different view of liberty.

Life in 1961 will not be easy. Wishing it, predicting it, even asking for it, will not make it so. There will be further setbacks before the tide is turned. But turn it we must. The hopes of all mankind rest upon us - not simply upon those of us in this chamber, but upon the peasant in Laos, the fisherman in Nigeria, the exile from Cuba, the spirit that moves every man and Nation who shares our hopes for freedom and the future. And in the final analysis, they rest most of all upon the pride and perseverance of our fellow citizens of the great Republic.

In the words of a great President, whose birthday we honor today, closing his final State of the Union Message sixteen years ago, "We pray that we may be worthy of the unlimited opportunities that God has given us."

The Peace Corps
A Special Message To The Congress
Washington, DC
March 1, 1961

I recommend to the Congress the establishment of a permanent Peace Corps - a pool of trained American men and women sent overseas by the U.S. Government or through private organizations and institutions to help foreign countries meet their urgent needs for skilled manpower. I have today signed an Executive Order establishing a Peace Corps on a temporary pilot basis.

The temporary Peace Corps will be a source of information and experience to aid us in formulating more effective plans for a permanent organization. In addition, by starting the Peace Corps now we will be able to begin training young men and women for overseas duty this summer with the objective of placing them in overseas positions by late fall. This temporary Peace Corps is being established under existing authority in the Mutual Security Act and will be located in the Department of State. Its initial expenses will be paid from appropriations currently available for our foreign aid program.

Throughout the world the people of the newly developing nations are struggling for economic and social progress which reflects their deepest desires. Our own freedom, and the future of freedom around the world, depend, in a very real sense, on their ability to build growing and independent nations where men can live in dignity, liberated from the bonds of hunger, ignorance and poverty.

One of the greatest obstacles to the achievement of this goal is the lack of trained men and women with the skill to teach the young and assist in the operation of development projects - men and women with the capacity to cope with the demands of swiftly evolving economies, and with the dedication to put that capacity to work in the villages, the mountains, the towns and the factories of dozens of struggling nations.

The vast task of economic development urgently requires skilled people to do the work of the society - to help teach in the schools, construct development projects, demonstrate modern methods of sanitation in the villages, and perform a hundred other tasks calling for training and advanced knowledge.

To meet this urgent need for skilled manpower we are proposing the establishment of a Peace Corps - an organization which will recruit and train American volunteers, sending them abroad to work with the people of other nations.

This organization will differ from existing assistance programs in that its members will supplement technical advisers by offering the specific skills needed by developing nations if they are to put technical advice to work. They will help provide the skilled manpower necessary to carry out the development projects planned by the host governments, acting at a working level and serving at great personal sacrifice. There is little doubt that the number of those who wish to serve will be far greater than our capacity to absorb them.

The Peace Corps or some similar approach has been strongly advocated by Senator Humphrey, Representative

Reuss and others in the Congress. It has received strong support from universities, voluntary agencies, student groups, labor unions and business and professional organizations.

Last session, the Congress authorized a study of these possibilities. Preliminary reports of this study show that the Peace Corps is feasible, needed, and wanted by many foreign countries.

Most heartening of all, the initial reaction to this proposal has been an enthusiastic response by student groups, professional organizations and private citizens everywhere - a convincing demonstration that we have in this country an immense reservoir of dedicated men and women willing to devote their energies and time and toil to the cause of world peace and human progress.

Among the specific programs to which Peace Corps members can contribute are: teaching in primary and secondary schools, especially as part of national English language teaching programs; participation in the worldwide program of malaria eradication; instruction and operation of public health and sanitation projects; aiding in village development through school construction and other programs; increasing rural agricultural productivity by assisting local farmers to use modern implements and techniques. The initial emphasis of these programs will be on teaching. Thus the Peace Corps members will be an effective means of implementing the development programs of the host countries - programs which our technical assistance operations have helped to formulate.

The Peace Corps will not be limited to the young, or to college graduates. All Americans who are qualified will be welcome to join this effort. But undoubtedly the Corps will be made up primarily of young people as they complete their formal education.

Because one of the greatest resources of a free society is the strength and diversity of its private organizations and institutions much of the Peace Corps program will be carried out by these groups, financially assisted by the Federal Government.

Peace Corps personnel will be made available to developing nations in the following ways:

1. Through private voluntary agencies carrying on international assistance programs.

2. Through overseas programs of colleges and universities.

3. Through assistance programs of international agencies.

4. Through assistance programs of the United States government.

5. Through new programs which the Peace Corps itself directly administers.

In the majority of cases the Peace Corps will assume the entire responsibility for recruitment, training and the development of overseas projects. In other cases, it will make available a pool of trained applicants to private groups who are carrying out projects approved by the Peace Corps.

In the case of Peace Corps programs conducted through voluntary agencies and universities, these private institutions will have the option of using the national recruitment system - the central pool of trained manpower - or developing recruitment systems of their own.

In all cases men and women recruited as a result of Federal assistance will be members of the Peace Corps and enrolled in the central organization. All private recruitment and training programs will adhere to Peace Corps standards as a condition of Federal assistance.

In all instances the men and women of the Peace Corps will go only to those countries where their services and skills are genuinely needed and desired. U.S. Operations Missions, supplemented where necessary by special Peace Corps teams, will consult with leaders in foreign countries in order to determine where Peace Corpsmen are needed, the types of job they can best fill, and the number of people who can be usefully employed. The Peace Corps will not supply personnel for marginal undertakings without a sound economic or social justification. In furnishing assistance through the Peace Corps careful regard will be given to the particular country's developmental priorities.

Membership in the Peace Corps will be open to all Americans, and applications will be available shortly. Where application is made directly to the Peace Corps - the vast majority of cases - they will be carefully screened to make sure that those who are selected can contribute to Peace Corps programs, and have the personal qualities which will enable them to represent the United States abroad with honor and dignity. In those cases where application is made directly to a private group, the same basic standards will be maintained. Each new recruit will receive a training and orientation period varying from six weeks to six months. This training will include courses in the culture and language of the country to which they are being sent and specialized training designed to increase the work skills of recruits. In some cases training will be conducted by participant agencies and universities in approved training programs. Other training programs will be conducted by the Peace Corps staff.

Length of service in the Corps will vary depending on the kind of project and the country, generally ranging from two to three years. Peace Corps members will often serve under conditions of physical hardship, living under primitive conditions among the people of developing nations. For every Peace Corps member service will mean a great financial sacrifice. They will receive no salary. Instead they will be given an allowance which will only be sufficient to meet their basic needs and maintain health. It is essential that Peace Corpsmen and women live simply and unostentatiously among the people they have come to assist. At the conclusion of their tours, members of the Peace Corps will receive a small sum in the form of severance pay based on length of service abroad, to assist them during their first weeks back in the United States. Service with the Peace Corps will not exempt volunteers from Selective Service.

The United States will assume responsibility for supplying medical services to Peace Corps members and ensuring supplies and drugs necessary to good health.

I have asked the temporary Peace Corps to begin plans and make arrangements for pilot programs. A minimum of several hundred volunteers could be selected, trained and at work abroad by the end of this calendar year. It is hoped that within a few years several thousand Peace Corps members will be working in foreign lands.

It is important to remember that this program must, in its early stages, be experimental in nature. This is a new dimension in our overseas program and only the most careful planning and negotiation can ensure its success.

The benefits of the Peace Corps will not be limited to the countries in which it serves. Our own young men and women will be enriched by the experience of living and working in foreign lands. They will have acquired new skills and experience which will aid them in their future careers and add to our own country's supply of trained personnel and teachers. They will return better able to assume the responsibilities of American citizenship and with greater understanding of our global responsibilities.

Although this is an American Peace Corps, the problem of world development is not just an American problem. Let us hope that other nations will mobilize the spirit and energies and skill of their people in some form of Peace Corps - making our own effort only one step in a major international effort to increase the welfare of all men and improve understanding among nations.

The Bay of Pigs
A Letter to Nikita Krushchev
Washington, DC
April 18, 1961

You are under a serious misapprehension in regard to events in Cuba. For months there has been evident and growing resistance to the Castro dictatorship. More than 100,000 refugees have recently fled from Cuba into neighboring countries. Their urgent hope is naturally to assist their fellow Cubans in their struggle for freedom. Many of these refugees fought alongside Dr. Castro against the Batista dictatorship; among them are prominent leaders of his own original movement and government.

These are unmistakable signs that Cubans find intolerable the denial of democratic liberties and the subversion of the 26th of July Movement by an alien-dominated regime. It cannot be surprising that, as resistance within Cuba grows, refugees have been using whatever means are available to return and support their countrymen in the continuing struggle for freedom. Where people are denied the right of choice, recourse to such struggle is the only means of achieving their liberties.

I have previously stated, and I repeat now, that the United States intends no military intervention in Cuba. In the event of any military intervention by outside force we will immediately honor our obligations under the inter-American system to protect this hemisphere against external aggression. While refraining from military intervention in Cuba, the people of the United States do not conceal their admiration for Cuban patriots who wish to see a democratic system in an independent Cuba. The United States government can take no action to stifle the spirit of liberty.

I have taken careful note of your statement that the events in Cuba might affect peace in all parts of the world. I trust that this does not mean that the Soviet government, using the situation in Cuba as a pretext, is planning to inflame other areas of the world. I would like to think that your government has too great a sense of responsibility to embark upon any enterprise so dangerous to general peace.

I agree with you as to the desirability of steps to improve the international atmosphere. I continue to hope that you will cooperate in opportunities now available to this end. A prompt ceasefire and peaceful settlement of the dangerous situation in Laos, cooperation with the United Nations in the Congo and a speedy conclusion of an acceptable treaty for the banning of nuclear tests would be constructive steps in this direction. The regime in Cuba could make a similar contribution by permitting the Cuban people freely to determine their own future by democratic processes and freely to cooperate with their Latin American neighbors.

I believe, Mr. Chairman, that you should recognize that free peoples in all parts of the world do not accept the claim of historical inevitability for the Communist revolution. What your government believes is its own business; what it does in the world is the world's business. The great revolution in the history of man, past, present and future, is the revolution of those determined to be free.

The President and the Press
An Address Before the American Newspaper Publishers Association
New York City
April 27, 1961

I appreciate very much your generous invitation to be here tonight.

You bear heavy responsibilities these days and an article I read some time ago reminded me of how particularly heavily the burdens of present day events bear upon your profession.

You may remember that in 1851 the *New York Herald Tribune*, under the sponsorship and publishing of Horace Greeley, employed as its London correspondent an obscure journalist by the name of Karl Marx.

We are told that foreign correspondent Marx, stone broke, and with a family ill and undernourished, constantly appealed to Greeley and Managing Editor Charles Dana for an increase in his munificent salary of $5 per installment, a salary which he and Engels ungratefully labeled as the "lousiest petty bourgeois cheating."

But when all his financial appeals were refused, Marx looked around for other means of livelihood and fame, eventually terminating his relationship with the *Tribune* and devoting his talents full time to the cause that would bequeath to the world the seeds of Leninism, Stalinism, revolution and the cold war.

If only this capitalistic New York newspaper had treated him more kindly; if only Marx had remained a foreign correspondent, history might have been different. And I hope all publishers will bear this lesson in mind the next time they receive a poverty-stricken appeal for a small increase in the expense account from an obscure newspaper man.

I have selected as the title of my remarks tonight "The President and the Press." Some may suggest that this would be more naturally worded "The President Versus the Press." But those are not my sentiments tonight.

It is true, however, that when a well-known diplomat from another country demanded recently that our State Department repudiate certain newspaper attacks on his colleague it was unnecessary for us to reply that this Administration was not responsible for the press, for the press had already made it clear that it was not responsible for this Administration.

Nevertheless, my purpose here tonight is not to deliver the usual assault on the so-called one-party press. On the contrary, in recent months I have rarely heard any complaints about political bias in the press except from a few Republicans. Nor is it my purpose tonight to discuss or defend the televising of Presidential press conferences. I think it is highly beneficial to have some 20,000,000 Americans regularly sit in on these conferences to observe, if I may say so, the incisive, the intelligent and the courteous qualities displayed by your Washington correspondents.

Nor, finally, are these remarks intended to examine the proper degree of privacy which the press should allow to any President and his family. If in the last few months your White House reporters and photographers have been attending church services with regularity, that has surely done them no harm.

On the other hand, I realize that your staff and wire service photographers may be complaining that they do not enjoy the same green privileges at the local golf courses which they once did.

It is true that my predecessor did not object as I do to pictures of one's golfing skill in action. But neither on the other hand did he ever bean a Secret Service man.

My topic tonight is a more sober one of concern to publishers as well as editors.

I want to talk about our common responsibilities in the face of a common danger. The events of recent weeks may have helped to illuminate that challenge for some; but the dimensions of its threat have loomed large on the horizon for many years. Whatever our hopes may be for the future - for reducing this threat or living with it - there is no escaping either the gravity or the totality of its challenge to our survival and to our security - a challenge that confronts us in unaccustomed ways in every sphere of human activity.

This deadly challenge imposes upon our society two requirements of direct concern both to the press and to the President - two requirements that may seem almost contradictory in tone, but which must be reconciled and fulfilled if we are to meet this national peril. I refer, *first*, to the need for far greater public information; and, *second*, to the need for far greater official secrecy.

The very word "secrecy" is repugnant in a free and open society; and we are as a people inherently and historically opposed to secret societies, to secret oaths and to secret proceedings. We decided long ago that the dangers of excessive and unwarranted concealment of pertinent facts far outweighed the dangers which are cited to justify it. Even today, there is little value in opposing the threat of a closed society by imitating its arbitrary restrictions. Even today, there is little value in insuring the survival of our nation if our traditions do not survive with it. And there is very grave danger that an announced need for increased security will be seized upon by those anxious to expand its meaning to the very limits of official censorship and concealment. That I do not intend to permit to the extent that it is in my control. And no official of my Administration, whether his rank is high or low, civilian or military, should interpret my words here tonight as an excuse to censor the news, to stifle dissent, to cover up our mistakes or to withhold from the press and the public the facts they deserve to know.

But I do ask every publisher, every editor, and every newsman in the nation to reexamine his own standards, and to recognize the nature of our country's peril. In time of war, the government and the press have customarily joined in an effort, based largely on self-discipline, to prevent unauthorized disclosures to the enemy. In time of "clear and present danger," the courts have held that even the privileged rights of the First Amendment must yield to the public's need for national security.

Today no war has been declared - and however fierce the struggle may be, it may never be declared in the traditional fashion. Our way of life is under attack.

Those who make themselves our enemy are advancing around the globe. The survival of our friends is in danger. And yet no war has been declared, no borders have been crossed by marching troops, no missiles have been fired.

If the press is awaiting a declaration of war before it imposes the self-discipline of combat conditions, then I can only say that no war ever posed a greater threat to our security. If you are awaiting a finding of "clear and present danger," then I can only say that the danger has never been more clear and its presence has never been more imminent.

It requires a change in outlook, a change in tactics, a change in missions - by the government, by the people, by every businessman or labor leader, and by every newspaper. For we are opposed around the world by a monolithic and ruthless conspiracy that relies primarily on covert means for expanding its sphere of influence - on infiltration instead of invasion, on subversion instead of elections, on intimidation instead of free choice, on guerrillas by night instead of armies by day. It is a system which has conscripted vast human and material resources into the building of a tightly knit, highly efficient machine that combines military, diplomatic, intelligence, economic, scientific and political operations.

Its preparations are concealed, not published. Its mistakes are buried, not headlined. Its dissenters are silenced, not praised. No expenditure is questioned, no rumor is printed, no secret is revealed. It conducts the Cold War, in short, with a war-time discipline no democracy would ever hope or wish to match.

Nevertheless, every democracy recognizes the necessary restraints of national security - and the question remains whether those restraints need to be more strictly observed if we are to oppose this kind of attack as well as outright invasion.

For the facts of the matter are that this nation's foes have openly boasted of acquiring through our newspapers information they would otherwise hire agents to acquire through theft, bribery or espionage; that details of this nation's covert preparations to counter the enemy's covert operations have been available to every newspaper reader, friend and foe alike; that the size, the strength, the location and the nature of our forces and weapons, and our plans and strategy for their use, have all been pinpointed in the press and other news media to a degree sufficient to satisfy any foreign power; and that, in at least one case, the publication of details concerning a secret mechanism whereby satellites were followed required its alteration at the expense of considerable time and money.

The newspapers which printed these stories were loyal, patriotic, responsible and well-meaning. Had we been engaged in open warfare, they undoubtedly would not have published such items. But in the absence of open warfare, they recognized only the tests of journalism and not the tests of national security. And my question tonight is whether additional tests should not now be adopted.

That question is for you alone to answer. No public official should answer it for you. No governmental plan should impose its restraints against your will. But I would be failing in my duty to the Nation, in considering all of the responsibilities that we now bear and all of the means at hand to meet those responsibilities, if I did not commend this problem to your attention, and urge its thoughtful consideration.

On many earlier occasions, I have said - and your newspapers have constantly said - that these are times that appeal to every citizen's sense of sacrifice and self-discipline. They call out to every citizen to weigh his rights and comforts against his obligations to the common good. I cannot now believe that those citizens who serve in the newspaper business consider themselves exempt from that appeal.

I have no intention of establishing a new Office of War Information to govern the flow of news. I am not suggesting any new forms of censorship or new types of security classifications. I have no easy answer to the dilemma that I have posed, and would not seek to impose it if I had one. But I am asking the members of the newspaper profession and the industry in this country to reexamine their own responsibilities, to consider the degree and the nature of the present danger, and to heed the duty of self-restraint which that danger imposes upon us all.

Every newspaper now asks itself, with respect to every story: "Is it news?" All I suggest is that you add the question: "Is it in the interest of the national security?" And I hope that every group in America - unions and businessmen and public officials at every level - will ask the same question of their endeavors, and subject their actions to this same exacting test.

And should the press of America consider and recommend the voluntary assumption of specific new steps or machinery, I can assure you that we will cooperate wholeheartedly with those recommendations.

Perhaps there will be no recommendations. Perhaps there is no answer to the dilemma faced by a free and open society in a cold and secret war. In times of peace, any discussion of this subject, and any action that results, are both painful and without precedent. But this is a time of peace and peril which knows no precedent in history.

It is the unprecedented nature of this challenge that also gives rise to your second obligation - an obligation which I share. And that is our obligation to inform and alert the American people - to make certain that they possess all the facts that they need, and understand them as well the perils, the prospects, the purposes of our program and the choices that we face.

No President should fear public scrutiny of his program. For from that scrutiny comes understanding; and from that understanding comes support or opposition. And both are necessary. I am not asking your newspapers to support the Administration, but I am asking your help in the tremendous task of informing and alerting the American people. For I have complete confidence in the response and dedication of our citizens whenever they are fully informed.

I not only could not stifle controversy among your readers - I welcome it. This Administration intends to be candid about its errors; for, as a wise man once said: "An error doesn't become a mistake until you refuse to correct it."

We intend to accept full responsibility for our errors; and we expect you to point them out when we miss them.

Without debate, without criticism, no Administration and no country can succeed - and no republic can survive. That is why the Athenian law-maker Solon decreed it a crime for any citizen to shrink from controversy. And that is why our press was protected by the First Amendment - the only business in America specifically protected by the Constitution - not primarily to amuse and entertain, not to emphasize the trivial and the sentimental, not to simply "give the public what it wants" - but to inform, to arouse, to reflect, to state our dangers and our opportunities, to indicate our crises and our choices, to lead, mold, educate and sometimes even anger public opinion.

This means greater coverage and analysis of international news - for it is no longer far away and foreign but close at hand and local. It means greater attention to improved understanding of the news as well as improved transmission. And it means, finally, that government at all levels, must meet its obligation to provide you with the fullest possible information outside the narrowest limits of national security - and we intend to do it.

It was early in the Seventeenth Century that Francis Bacon remarked on three recent inventions already transforming the world: the compass, gunpowder and the printing press. Now the links between the nations first forged by the compass have made us all citizens of the world, the hopes and threats of one becoming the hopes and threats of us all. In that one world's efforts to live together, the evolution of gunpowder to its ultimate limit has warned mankind of the terrible consequences of failure.

And so it is to the printing press - to the recorder of man's deeds, the keeper of his conscience, the courier of his news - that we look for strength and assistance, confident that with your help man will be what he was born to be: free and independent.

Return From Europe
Washington, DC
June 6, 1961

I returned this morning from a week-long trip to Europe and I want to report to you on that trip in full. It was in every sense an unforgettable experience. The people of Paris, of Vienna, of London, were generous in their greeting. They were heartwarming in their hospitality, and their graciousness to my wife is particularly appreciated.

We knew of course that the crowds and the shouts were meant in large measure for the country that we represented, which is regarded as the chief defender of freedom. Equally memorable was the pageantry of European history and their culture that is very much a part of any ceremonial reception, to lay a wreath at the Arc de Triomphe, to dine at Versailles, and Schonbrunn Palace, and with the Queen of England. These are the colorful memories that will remain with us for many years to come. Each of the three cities that we visited - Paris, Vienna, and London - have existed for many centuries, and each serves as a reminder that the Western civilization that we seek to preserve has flowered over many years, and has defended itself over many centuries. But this was not a ceremonial trip. Two aims of American foreign policy, above all others, were the reason for the trip: the unity of the free world, whose strength is the security of us all, and the eventual achievement of a lasting peace. My trip was devoted to the advancement of these two aims.

To strengthen the unity of the West, our journey opened in Paris and closed in London. My talks with General de

Gaulle were profoundly encouraging to me. Certain differences in our attitudes on one or another problem became insignificant in view of our common commitment to defend freedom. Our alliance, I believe, became more secure; the friendship of our nation, I hope - with theirs - became firmer; and the relations between the two of us who bear responsibility became closer, and I hope were marked by confidence. I found General de Gaulle far more interested in our frankly stating our position, whether or not it was his own, than in appearing to agree with him when we do not. But he knows full well the true meaning of an alliance. He is after all the only major leader of World War II who still occupies a position of great responsibility. His life has been one of unusual dedication; he is a man of extraordinary personal character, symbolizing the new strength and the historic grandeur of France. Throughout our discussions he took the long view of France and the world at large. I found him a wise counselor for the future, and an informative guide to the history that he has helped to make. Thus we had a valuable meeting.

I believe that certain doubts and suspicions that might have come up in a long time - I believe were removed on both sides. Problems which proved to be not of substance but of wording or procedure were cleared away. No question, however sensitive, was avoided. No area of interest was ignored, and the conclusions that we reached will be important for the future - in our agreement on defending Berlin, on working to improve the defenses of Europe, on aiding the economic and political independence of the underdeveloped world, including Latin America, on spurring European economic unity, on concluding successfully the conference on Laos, and on closer consultations and solidarity in the Western alliance.

General de Gaulle could not have been more cordial, and I could not have more confidence in any man. In addition to his individual strength of character, the French people as a whole showed vitality and energy which were both impressive and gratifying. Their recovery from the postwar period is dramatic, their productivity is increasing, and they are steadily building their stature in both Europe and Africa, and thus, I left Paris for Vienna with increased confidence in Western unity and strength.

The people of Vienna know what it is to live under occupation, and they know what it is to live in freedom. Their welcome to me as President of this country should be heartwarming to us all. I went to Vienna to meet the leader of the Soviet Union, Mr. Khrushchev. For 2 days we met in sober, intensive conversation, and I believe it is my obligation to the people, to the Congress, and to our allies to report on those conversations candidly and publicly.

Mr. Khrushchev and I had a very full and frank exchange of views on the major issues that now divide our two countries. I will tell you now that is was a very sober two days. There was no discourtesy, no loss of tempers, no threats or ultimatums by either side; no advantage or concession was either gained or given; no major decision was either planned or taken; no spectacular progress was either achieved or pretended.

This kind of informal exchange may not be as exciting as a full-fledged summit meeting with a fixed agenda and a large corps of advisers, where negotiations are attempted and new agreements sought, but this was not intended to be and was not such a meeting, nor did we plan any future summit meetings at Vienna.

But I found this meeting with Chairman Khrushchev, as somber as it was, to be immensely useful, I had read his speeches and of his policies. I had been advised on his views. I had been told by other leaders of the West, General de Gaulle, Chancellor Adenauer, Prime Minister Macmillan, what manner of man he was.

But I bear the responsibility of the Presidency of the United States, and it is my duty to make decisions that no adviser and no ally can make for me. It is my obligation and responsibility to see that these decisions are as informed as possible, that they are based on as much direct, firsthand knowledge as possible.

I therefore thought it was of immense importance that I know Mr. Khrushchev, that I gain as much insight and understanding as I could on his present and future policies. At the same time, I wanted to make certain Mr. Khrushchev knew this country and its policies, that he understood our strength and our determination, and that he knew that we desired peace with all nations of every kind.

I wanted to present our views to him directly, precisely, realistically, and with an opportunity for discussion and clarification. This was done. No new aims were stated in private that have not been stated in public on either side. The gap between us was not, in such a short period, materially reduced, but at least the channels of communications were opened more fully, at least the chances of a dangerous misjudgment on either side should now be less, and at least the men on whose decisions the peace in part depends have agreed to remain in contact.

This is important, for neither of us tried to merely please the other, to agree merely to be agreeable, to say what the other wanted to hear. And just as our judicial system relies on witnesses appearing in court and on cross-examination, instead of hearsay testimony or affidavits on paper, so, too, was this direct give-and-take of immeasurable value in making clear and precise what we considered to be vital, for the facts of the matter are that the Soviets and ourselves give wholly different meanings to the same words - war, peace, democracy, and popular will.

We have wholly different views of right and wrong, of what is an internal affair and what is aggression, and, above all, we have wholly different concepts of where the world is and where it is going.

Only by such a discussion was it possible for me to be sure that Mr. Khrushchev knew how differently we view the present and the future. Our views contrasted sharply but at least we knew better at the end where we both stood. Neither of us was there to dictate a settlement or to convert the other to a cause or to concede our basic interests. But both of us were there, I think, because we realized that each nation has the power to inflict enormous damage upon the other, that such a war could and should be avoided if at all possible, since it would settle no dispute and prove no doctrine, and that care should thus be taken to prevent our conflicting interests from so directly confronting each other that war necessarily ensued. We believe in a system of national freedom and independence. He believes in an expanding and dynamic concept of world communism, and the question was whether these two systems can ever hope to live in peace without permitting any loss of security or any denial of the freedom of our friends. However difficult it may seem to answer this question in the affirmative as we approach so many harsh tests, I think we owe it to all mankind to make every possible effort. That is why I considered the Vienna talks to be useful. The somber mood that they conveyed was not cause for elation or relaxation, nor was it cause for undue pessimism or fear. It simply demonstrated how much work we in the free world have to do and how long and hard a struggle must be our fate as Americans in this generation as the chief defenders of the cause of liberty. The one area which afforded some immediate prospect of accord was Laos. Both sides recognized the need to reduce the dangers in that situation. Both sides endorsed the concept of a neutral and independent Laos, much in the manner of Burma or Cambodia.

Of critical importance to the current conference on Laos in Geneva, both sides recognized the importance of an effective ceasefire. It is urgent that this be translated into new attitudes at Geneva, enabling the International Control Commission to do its duty, to make certain that a ceasefire is enforced and maintained. I am hopeful that progress can be made on this matter in the coming days at Geneva for that would greatly improve international atmosphere.

No such hope emerged, however, with respect to the other deadlocked Geneva conference, seeking a treaty to ban nuclear tests. Mr. Khrushchev made it clear that there could not be a neutral administrator - in his opinion because no one was truly neutral; that a Soviet veto would have to apply to acts of enforcement; that inspection was only a subterfuge for espionage, in the absence of total disarmament; and that the present test ban negotiations appeared futile. In short, our hopes for an end to nuclear tests, for an end to the spread of nuclear weapons, and for some slowing down of the arms race have been struck a serious blow. Nevertheless, the stakes are too important for us to abandon the draft treaty we have offered at Geneva.

But our most somber talks were on the subject of Germany and Berlin. I made it clear to Mr. Khrushchev that the security of Western Europe and therefore our own security are deeply involved in our presence and our access rights to West Berlin, that those rights are based on law and not on sufferance, and that we are determined to maintain those rights at any risk, and thus meet our obligation to the people of West Berlin, and their right to choose their own future.

Mr. Khrushchev, in turn, presented his views in detail, and his presentation will be the subject of further communications. But we are not seeking to change the present situation. A binding Germany peace treaty is a matter for all who were at war with Germany, and we and our allies cannot abandon our obligations to the people of West Berlin.

Generally, Mr. Khrushchev did not talk in terms of war. He believes the world will move his way without resort to force. He spoke of his nation's achievements in space. He stressed his intention to outdo us in industrial production, to outtrade us, to prove to the world the superiority of his system over ours. Most of all, he predicted the triumph of communism in the new and less developed countries.

He was certain that the tide there was moving his way, that the revolution of rising peoples would eventually be a Communist revolution, and that the so-called wars of liberation, supported by the Kremlin, would replace the old methods of direct aggression and invasion.

In the 1940's and early fifties, the great danger was from Communist armies marching across free borders, which we saw in Korea. Our nuclear monopoly helped to prevent this in other areas. Now we face a new and different threat. We no longer have a nuclear monopoly. Their missiles, they believe, will hold off our missiles, and their troops can match our troops should we intervene in these so-called wars of liberation. Thus, the local conflict they support can turn in their favor through guerrillas or insurgents or subversion. A small group of disciplined Communists could exploit discontent and misery in a country where the average income may be $60 or $70 a year, and seize control, therefore, of an entire country without Communist troops ever crossing any international frontier. This is the Communist theory.

But I believe just as strongly that time will prove it wrong, that liberty and independence and self-determination - not communism - is the future of man, and that free men have the will and the resources to win the struggle for freedom. But it is clear that this struggle in this area of the new and poorer nations will be a continuing crisis of this decade.

Mr. Khrushchev made one point which I wish to pass on. He said there are many disorders throughout the world, and he should not be blamed for them all. He is quite right. It is easy to dismiss as Communist-inspired every anti-government or anti-American riot, every overthrow of a corrupt regime, or every mass protest against misery and despair. These are not all Communist-inspired. The

Communists move in to exploit them, to infiltrate their leadership, to ride their crest to victory. But the Communists did not create the conditions which caused them.

In short, the hopes for freedom in these areas which see so much poverty and illiteracy, so many children who are sick, so many children who die in the first year, so many families without homes, so many families without hope - the future for freedom in these areas rests with the local peoples and their governments.

If they have the will to determine their own future, if their governments have the support of their own people, if their honest and progressive measures - helping their people - have inspired confidence and zeal, then no guerrilla or insurgent action can succeed. But where those conditions do not exist, a military guarantee against external attack from across a border offers little protection against internal decay.

Yet all this does not mean that our Nation and the West and the free world can only sit by. On the contrary, we have an historic opportunity to help these countries build their societies until they are so strong and broadly based that only an outside invasion could topple them, and that threat, we know, can be stopped.

We can train and equip their forces to resist Communist-supplied insurrections. We can help develop the industrial and agricultural base on which new living standards can be built. We can encourage better administration and better education and better tax and land distribution and a better life for the people.

All this and more we can do because we have the talent and the resources to do it, if we will only use and share them. I know that there is a great deal of feeling in the United States that we have carried the burden of economic assistance long enough, but these countries that we are now supporting - stretching all the way along from the top of Europe through the Middle East, down through Saigon - are now subject to great efforts internally, in many of them, to seize control.

If we're not prepared to assist them in making a better life for their people, then I believe that the prospects for freedom in those areas are uncertain. We must, I believe, assist them if we are determined to meet with commitments of assistance our words against the Communist advance. The burden is heavy; we have carried it for many years. But I believe that this fight is not over. This battle goes on, and we have to play our part in it. And therefore I hope again that we will assist these people so that they can remain free.

It was fitting that Congress opened its hearings on our new foreign military and economic aid programs in Washington at the very time that Mr. Khrushchev's words in Vienna were demonstrating as nothing else could the need for that very program. It should be well run, effectively administered, but I believe we must do it, and I hope that you, the American people, will support it again, because I think it's vitally important to the security of these areas. There is no use talking against the Communist advance unless we're willing to meet our responsibilities, however burdensome they may be.

I do not justify this aid merely on the grounds of anti-Communism. It is a recognition of our opportunity and obligation to help those people be free, and we are not alone.

I found that the people of France, for example, were doing far more in Africa in the way of aiding independent nations than our own country was. But I know that foreign aid is a burden that is keenly felt and I can only say that we have no more crucial obligation now.

My stay in England was short but the visit gave me a chance to confer privately again with Prime Minister Macmillan, just as others of our party in Vienna were conferring yesterday with General de Gaulle and Chancellor Adenauer. We all agreed that there is work to be done in the West and from our conversations have come agreed steps to get on with that work. Our day in London, capped by a meeting with Queen Elizabeth and Prince Philip was a strong reminder at the end of a long journey that the West remains united in its determination to hold to its standards.

May I conclude by saying simply that I am glad to be home. We have on this trip admired splendid places and seen stirring sights, but we are glad to be home. No demonstration of support abroad could mean so much as the support which you, the American people, have so generously given to our country. With that support I am not fearful of the future. We must be patient. We must be determined. We must be courageous. We must accept both risks and burdens, but with the will and the work freedom will prevail.

Commencement Address
United States Naval Academy
Annapolis, Maryland
June 7, 1961

I am proud as a citizen of the United States to come to this institution and this room where there is concentrated so many men who have committed themselves to the defense of the United States. I am honored to be here.

In the past I have had some slight contact with this Service, though I never did reach the state of professional and physical perfection where I could hope that anyone would ever mistake me for an Annapolis graduate.

I know that you are constantly warned during your days here not to mix, in your Naval career, in politics. I should point out, however, on the other side, that my rather rapid rise from a Reserve Lieutenant, of uncertain standing, to Commander-in-Chief, has been because I did not follow that very good advice.

I trust, however, that those of you who are Regulars will, for a moment, grant a retired civilian officer some measure of fellowship.

Nearly a half century ago, President Woodrow Wilson came here to Annapolis on a similar mission, and addressed the Class of 1914. On that day, the graduating class numbered 154 men. There has been, since that time, a revolution in the size of our military establishment, and that revolution has been reflected in the revolution in the world around us.

When Wilson addressed the class in 1914, the Victorian structure of power was still intact, the world was dominated by Europe, and Europe itself was the scene of an uneasy balance of power between dominant figures and America was a spectator on a remote sideline.

The autumn after Wilson came to Annapolis, the Victorian world began to fall to pieces, and our world one-half a century later is vastly different. Today we are witnesses to the most extraordinary revolution, nearly, in the history of the world, as the emergent nations of Latin America, Africa, and Asia awaken from long centuries of torpor and impatience.

Today the Victorian certitudes which were taken to be so much a part of man's natural existence are under siege by a faith committed to the destruction of liberal civilization, and today the United States is no longer the spectator, but the leader.

This half century, therefore, has not only revolutionized the size of our military establishment, it has brought about also a more striking revolution in the things that the Nation expects from the men in our Service.

Fifty years ago the graduates of the Naval Academy were expected to be seamen and leaders of men. They were reminded of the saying of John Paul Jones, "Give me a fair ship so that I might go into harm's way."

When Captain Mahan began to write in the nineties on the general issues of war and peace and naval strategy, the Navy quickly shipped him to sea duty. Today we expect all of you - in fact, you must, of necessity - be prepared not only to handle a ship in a storm or a landing party on a beach, but to make great determinations which affect the survival of this country.

The revolution in the technology of war makes it necessary in order that you, when you hold positions of command, may make an educated judgment between various techniques, that you also be a scientist and an engineer and a physicist, and your responsibilities go far beyond the classic problems of tactics and strategy.

In the years to come, some of you will serve as your Commandant did last year, as an adviser to foreign governments; some will negotiate as Admiral Burke did, in Korea, with other governments on behalf of the United States; some will go to the far reaches of space and some will go to the bottom of the ocean. Many of you from one time or another, in the positions of command, or as members of staff, will participate in great decisions which go far beyond the narrow reaches of professional competence.

You gentlemen, therefore, have a most important responsibility, to recognize that your education is just beginning, and to be prepared, in the most difficult period in the life of our country, to play the role that the country hopes and needs and expects from you. You must understand not only this country but other countries. You must know something about strategy and tactics and logic - logistics, but also economics and politics and diplomacy and history. You must know everything you can know about military power, and you must also understand the limits of military power. You must understand that few of the important problems of our time have, in the final analysis, been finally solved by military power alone. When I say that officers today must go far beyond the official curriculum, I say it not because I do not believe in the traditional relationship between the civilian and the military, but you must be more than the servants of national policy. You must be prepared to play a constructive role in the development of national policy, a policy which protects our interests and our security and the peace of the world. Woodrow Wilson reminded your predecessors that you were not serving a government or an administration, but a people. In serving the American people, you represent the American people and the best of the ideals of this free society. Your posture and your performance will provide many people far beyond our shores, who know very little of our country, the only evidence they will ever see as to whether America is truly dedicated to the cause of justice and freedom.

In my inaugural address, I said that each citizen should be concerned not with what his country can do for him, but what he can do for his country. What you have chosen to do for your country, by devoting your life to the service of our country, is the greatest contribution that any man could make. It is easy for you, in a moment of exhilaration today, to say that you freely and gladly dedicate your life to the United States. But the life of service is a constant test of your will.

It will be hard at times to face the personal sacrifice and the family inconvenience, to maintain this high resolve, to place the needs of your country above all else. When there is a visible enemy to fight, the tide of patriotism in this country runs strong. But when there is a long, slow struggle, with no immediate visible foe, when you watch your contemporaries indulging the urge for material gain and comfort and personal advancement, your choice will seem hard, and you will recall, I am sure, the lines found in the old sentry box at Gibraltar, "God and the soldier all men adore in time of trouble and no more, for when war is over, and all things righted, God is neglected and the old soldier slighted."

Never forget, however, that the battle for freedom takes many forms. Those who through vigilance and firmness and devotion are the great servants of this country - and let us have no doubt that the United States needs your devoted assistance today.

The answer to those who challenge us so severely in so many parts of the globe lies in our willingness to freely commit ourselves to the maintenance of our country and the things for which it stands.

This ceremony today represents the kind of commitment which you are willing to make. For that reason, I am proud to be here. This nation salutes you as you commence your service to our country in the hazardous days ahead. And on behalf of all of them, I congratulate you and thank you.

The Berlin Crisis
Radio and Television Address
Washington, DC
July 25, 1961

Seven weeks ago tonight I returned from Europe to report on my meeting with Premier Khrushchev and the others. His grim warnings about the future of the world, his aide memoire on Berlin, his subsequent speeches and threats which he and his agents have launched, and the increase in the Soviet military budget that he has announced, have all prompted a series of decisions by the Administration and a series of consultations with the members of the NATO organization. In Berlin, as you recall, he intends to bring to an end, through a stroke of the pen, *first* our legal rights to be in West Berlin - and *secondly* our ability to make good on our commitment to the two million free people of that city. That we cannot permit.

We are clear about what must be done - and we intend to do it. I want to talk frankly with you tonight about the first steps that we shall take. These actions will require sacrifice on the part of many of our citizens. More will be required in the future. They will require, from all of us, courage and perseverance in the years to come. But if we and our allies act out of strength and unity of purpose - with calm determination and steady nerves - using restraint in our words as well as our weapons - I am hopeful that both peace and freedom will be sustained.

The immediate threat to free men is in West Berlin. But that isolated outpost is not an isolated problem. The threat is worldwide. Our effort must be equally wide and strong, and not be obsessed by any single manufactured crisis. We face a challenge in Berlin, but there is also a challenge in Southeast Asia, where the borders are less guarded, the enemy harder to find, and the dangers of communism less apparent to those who have so little. We face a challenge in our own hemisphere, and indeed wherever else the freedom of human beings is at stake.

Let me remind you that the fortunes of war and diplomacy left the free people of West Berlin, in 1945, 110 miles behind the Iron Curtain.

This map makes very clear the problem that we face. The white is West Germany - the East is the area controlled by the Soviet Union, and as you can see from the chart, West Berlin is 110 miles within the area which the Soviets now dominate - which is immediately controlled by the so-called East German regime.

We are there as a result of our victory over Nazi Germany - and our basic rights to be there, deriving from that victory, include both our presence in West Berlin and the enjoyment of access across East Germany. These rights have been repeatedly confirmed and recognized in special agreements with the Soviet Union. Berlin is not a part of East Germany, but a separate territory under the control of the allied powers. Thus our rights there are clear and deep-rooted. But in addition to those rights is our commitment to sustain - and defend, if need be - the opportunity for more than two million people to determine their own future and choose their own way of life.

Thus our presence in West Berlin, and our access thereto, cannot be ended by any act of the Soviet government. The NATO shield was long ago extended to cover West

Berlin - and we have given our word that an attack upon that city will be regarded as an attack upon us all.

For West Berlin - lying exposed - 110 miles inside East Germany, surrounded by Soviet troops and close to Soviet supply lines, has many roles. It is more than a showcase of liberty, a symbol, an island of freedom in a Communist sea. It is even more than a link with the Free World, a beacon of hope behind the Iron Curtain, an escape hatch for refugees.

West Berlin is all of that. But above all it has now become - as never before - the great testing place of Western courage and will, a focal point where our solemn commitments stretching back over the years since 1945, and Soviet ambitions now meet in basic confrontation.

It would be a mistake for others to look upon Berlin, because of its location, as a tempting target. The United States is there; the United Kingdom and France are there; the pledge of NATO is there - and the people of Berlin are there. It is as secure, in that sense, as the rest of us - for we cannot separate its safety from our own.

I hear it said that West Berlin is militarily untenable. And so was Bastogne. And so, in fact, was Stalingrad. Any dangerous spot is tenable if men - brave men - will make it so.

We do not want to fight - but we have fought before. And others in earlier times have made the same dangerous mistake of assuming that the West was too selfish and too soft and too divided to resist invasions of freedom in other lands. Those who threaten to unleash the forces of war on a dispute over West Berlin should recall the words of the ancient philosopher: "A man who causes fear cannot be free from fear."

We cannot and will not permit the Communists to drive us out of Berlin, either gradually or by force. For the fulfillment of our pledge to that city is essential to the morale and security of Western Germany, to the unity of Western Europe, and to the faith of the entire Free World. Soviet strategy has long been aimed, not merely at Berlin, but at dividing and neutralizing all of Europe, forcing us back on our own shores. We must meet out oft-stated pledge to the free peoples of West Berlin - and maintain our rights and their safety, even in the face of force - in order to maintain the confidence of other free peoples in our word and our resolve. The strength of the alliance on which our security depends is dependent in turn on our willingness to meet our commitments to them.

So long as the Communists insist that they are preparing to end by themselves unilaterally our rights in West Berlin and our commitments to its people, we must be prepared to defend those rights and those commitments. We will at all times be ready to talk, if talk will help. But we must also be ready to resist with force, if force is used upon us. Either alone would fail. Together, they can serve the cause of freedom and peace.

The new preparations that we shall make to defend the peace are part of the long-term buildup in our strength which has been underway since January. They are based on our needs to meet a worldwide threat, on a basis which stretches far beyond the present Berlin crisis. Our primary purpose is neither propaganda nor provocation - but preparation.

A first need is to hasten progress toward the military goals which the North Atlantic allies have set for themselves. In Europe today nothing less will suffice. We will put even greater resources into fulfilling those goals, and we look to our allies to do the same.

The supplementary defense buildups that I asked from the Congress in March and May have already started moving us toward these and our other defense goals. They included an increase in the size of the Marine Corps, improved readiness of our reserves, expansion of our air and sea lift, and stepped-up procurement of needed weapons, ammunition, and other items. To insure a continuing invulnerable capacity to deter or destroy any aggressor, they provided for the strengthening of our missile power and for putting 50% of our B-52 and B-47 bombers on a ground alert which would send them on their way with 15 minutes' warning.

These measures must be speeded up, and still others must now be taken. We must have sea and air lift capable of moving our forces quickly and in large numbers to any part of the world.

But even more importantly, we need the capability of placing in any critical area at the appropriate time a force which, combined with those of our allies, is large enough to make clear our determination and our ability to defend our rights at all costs - and to meet all levels of aggressor pressure with whatever levels of force are required. We intend to have a wider choice than humiliation or all-out nuclear action.

While it is unwise at this time either to call up or send abroad excessive numbers of these troops before they are needed, let me make it clear that I intend to take, as time goes on, whatever steps are necessary to make certain that such forces can be deployed at the appropriate time without lessening our ability to meet our commitments elsewhere.

Thus, in the days and months ahead, I shall not hesitate to ask the Congress for additional measures, or exercise any of the executive powers that I possess to meet this threat to peace. Everything essential to the security of freedom must be done; and if that should require more men, or more taxes, or more controls, or other new powers, I shall not hesitate to ask them. The measures proposed today will be constantly studied, and altered as necessary. But while we will not let panic shape our policy, neither will we permit timidity to direct our program.

Accordingly, I am now taking the following steps:

I am tomorrow requesting the Congress for the current fiscal year an additional $3,247,000,000 of appropriations for the Armed Forces.

To fill out our present Army Divisions, and to make more men available for prompt deployment, I am requesting an increase in the Army's total authorized strength from 875,000 to approximately 1 million men.

I am requesting an increase of 29,000 and 63,000 men respectively in the active duty strength of the Navy and the Air Force.

To fulfill these manpower needs, I am ordering that our draft calls be doubled and tripled in the coming months; I am asking the Congress for authority to order to active duty certain ready reserve units and individual reservists, and to extend tours of duty; and, under that authority, I am planning to order to active duty a number of air transport squadrons and Air National Guard tactical air squadrons, to give us the airlift capacity and protection that we need. Other reserve forces will be called up when needed.

Many ships and planes once headed for retirement are to be retained or reactivated, increasing our airpower tactically and our sea lift, airlift, and anti-submarine warfare capability. In addition, our strategic air power will be increased by delaying the deactivation of B-47 bombers.

Finally, some $1.8 billion - about half of the total sum - is needed for the procurement of non-nuclear weapons, ammunition and equipment.

The details on all these requests will be presented to the Congress tomorrow. Subsequent steps will be taken to suit subsequent needs. Comparable efforts for the common defense are being discussed with our NATO allies. For their commitment and interest are as precise as our own.

And let me add that I am well aware of the fact that many American families will bear the burden of these requests. Studies or careers will be interrupted; husbands and sons will be called away; incomes in some cases will be reduced. But these are burdens which must be borne if freedom is to be defended - Americans have willingly borne them before - and they will not flinch from the task now.

We have another sober responsibility. To recognize the possibilities of nuclear war in the missile age, without our citizens knowing what they should do and where they should go if bombs begin to fall, would be a failure of responsibility. In May, I pledged a new start on Civil Defense. Last week, I assigned, on the recommendation of the Civil Defense Director, basic responsibility for this program to the Secretary of Defense, to make certain it is administered and coordinated with our continental defense efforts at the highest civilian level. Tomorrow, I am requesting of the Congress new funds for the following immediate objectives: to identify and mark space in existing structures - public and private - that could be used for fallout shelters in case of attack; to stock those shelters with food, water, first aid kits and other minimum essentials for survival; to increase their capacity; to improve our air-raid warning and fallout detection systems, including a new household warning system which is now under development; and to take other measures that will be effective at an early date to save millions of lives if needed.

In the event of an attack, the lives of those families which are not hit in a nuclear blast and fire can still be saved - *if* they can be warned to take shelter and *if* that shelter is available. We owe that kind of insurance to our families and to our country. In contrast to our friends in Europe, the need for this kind of protection is new to our shores. But the time to start is now. In the coming months, I hope to let every citizen know what steps he can take without delay to protect his family in case of attack. I know that you will want to do no less.

The addition of $207 million in Civil Defense appropriations brings our total new defense budget requests to $3.454 billion, and a total of $47.5 billion for the year. This is an increase in the defense budget of $6 billion since January, and has resulted in official estimates of a budget deficit of over $5 billion. The Secretary of the Treasury and other economic advisers assure me, however, that our economy has the capacity to bear this new request.

We are recovering strongly from this year's recession. The increase in this last quarter of our year of our total national output was greater than that for any postwar period of initial recovery. And yet, wholesale prices are actually lower than they were during the recession, and consumer prices are only 1/4 of 1% higher than they were last October. In fact, this last quarter was the first in eight years in which our production has increased without an increase in the overall price index. And for the first time since the fall of 1959, our gold position has improved and the dollar is more respected abroad. These gains, it should be stressed, are being accomplished with budget deficits far smaller than those of the 1958 recession.

This improved business outlook means improved revenues; and I intend to submit to the Congress in January a budget for the next fiscal year which will be strictly in balance. Nevertheless, should an increase in taxes be needed - because of events in the next few months - to achieve that balance, or because of subsequent defense rises, those increased taxes will be requested in January.

Meanwhile, to help make certain that the current deficit is held to a safe level, we must keep down all expenditures not thoroughly justified in budget requests. The luxury of our current post office deficit must be ended. Costs in military procurement will be closely scrutinized - and in this effort I welcome the cooperation of the Congress. The tax loopholes I have specified - on expense accounts, overseas income, dividends, interest, cooperatives and others - must be closed.

I realize that no public revenue measure is welcomed by everyone. But I am certain that every American wants to pay his fair share, and not leave the burden of defending freedom entirely to those who bear arms. For we have mortgaged our very future on this defense - and we cannot fail to meet our responsibilities.

But I must emphasize again that the choice is not merely between resistance and retreat, between atomic holocaust and surrender. Our peacetime military posture is traditionally defensive; but our diplomatic posture need not be. Our response to the Berlin crisis will not be merely military or negative. It will be more than merely standing firm. For we do not intend to leave it to others to choose and monopolize the forum and the framework of discussion. We do not intend to abandon our duty to mankind to seek a peaceful solution.

As signers of the UN Charter, we shall always be prepared to discuss international problems with any and all nations that are willing to talk - and listen - with reason. If they have proposals - not demands - we shall hear them. If they seek genuine understanding - not concessions of our rights - we shall meet with them. We have previously indicated our readiness to remove any actual irritants in West Berlin, but the freedom of that city is not negotiable. We cannot negotiate with those who say "What's mine is mine and what's yours is negotiable." But we are willing to consider any arrangement or treaty in Germany consistent with the maintenance of peace and freedom, and with the legitimate security interests of all nations.

We recognize the Soviet Union's historical concern about their security in Central and Eastern Europe, after a series of ravaging invasions, and we believe arrangements can be worked out which will help to meet those concerns, and make it possible for both security and freedom to exist in this troubled area.

For it is not the freedom of West Berlin which is "abnormal" in Germany today, but the situation in that entire divided country. If anyone doubts the legality of our rights in Berlin, we are ready to have it submitted to international adjudication. If anyone doubts the extent to which our presence is desired by the people of West Berlin, compared to East German feelings about their regime, we are ready to have that question submitted to a free vote in Berlin and, if possible, among all the German people. And let us hear at that time from the two and one-half million refugees who have fled the Communist regime in East Germany - voting for Western-type freedom with their feet.

The world is not deceived by the Communist attempt to label Berlin as a hotbed of war. There is peace in Berlin today. The source of world trouble and tension is Moscow, not Berlin. And if war begins, it will have begun in Moscow and not Berlin.

For the choice of peace or war is largely theirs, not ours. It is the Soviets who have stirred up this crisis. It is they who are trying to force a change. It is they who have opposed free elections. It is they who have rejected an all-German peace treaty, and the rulings of international law. And as Americans know from our history on our own old frontier, gun battles are caused by outlaws, and not by officers of the peace.

In short, while we are ready to defend our interests, we shall also be ready to search for peace - in quiet exploratory talks - in formal or informal meetings. We do not want military considerations to dominate the thinking of either East or West. And Mr. Khrushchev may find that his invitation to other nations to join in a meaningless treaty may lead to *their* inviting *him* to join in the community of peaceful men, in abandoning the use of force, and in respecting the sanctity of agreements.

While all of these efforts go on, we must not be diverted from our total responsibilities, from other dangers, from other tasks. If new threats in Berlin or elsewhere should cause us to weaken our program of assistance to the developing nations who are also under heavy pressure from the same source, or to halt our efforts for realistic disarmament, or to disrupt or slow down our economy, or to neglect the education of our children, then those threats will surely be the most successful and least costly maneuver in Communist history. For we can afford all these efforts, and more - but we cannot afford *not* to meet this challenge.

And the challenge is not to us alone. It is a challenge to every nation which asserts its sovereignty under a system of liberty. It is a challenge to all those who want a world of free choice. It is a special challenge to the Atlantic Community - the heartland of human freedom.

We in the West must move together in building military strength. We must consult one another more closely than ever before. We must together design our proposals for peace, and labor together as they are pressed at the conference table. And together we must share the burdens and the risks of this effort.

The Atlantic Community, as we know it, has been built in response to challenge: the challenge of European chaos in 1947, of the Berlin blockade in 1948, the challenge of Communist aggression in Korea in 1950. Now, standing strong and prosperous, after an unprecedented decade of progress, the Atlantic Community will not forget either its history or the principles which gave it meaning.

The solemn vow each of us gave to West Berlin in time of peace will not be broken in time of danger. If we do not meet our commitments to Berlin, where will we later stand? If we are not true to our word there, all that we have achieved in collective security, which relies on these words, will mean nothing. And if there is one path above all others to war, it is the path of weakness and disunity.

Today, the endangered frontier of freedom runs through divided Berlin. We want to remain a frontier of peace. This is the hope of every citizen of the Atlantic Community; every citizen of Eastern Europe; and, I am confident, every citizen of the Soviet Union. For I cannot believe that the Russian people - who bravely suffered enormous losses in the Second World War - would now wish to see the peace upset once more in Germany. The Soviet government alone can convert Berlin's frontier of peace into a pretext for war.

The steps I have indicated tonight are aimed at avoiding that war. To sum it all up: we seek peace - but we shall not surrender. That is the central meaning of this crisis, and the meaning of your government's policy.

With your help, and the help of other free men, this crisis can be surmounted. Freedom can prevail - and peace can endure.

I would like to close with a personal word. When I ran for the Presidency of the United States, I knew that this country faced serious challenges, but I could not realize - nor could any man realize who does not bear the burdens of this office - how heavy and constant would be those burdens.

Three times in my lifetime our country and Europe have been involved in major wars. In each case serious misjudgments were made on both sides of the intentions of others, which brought about great devastation.

Now, in the thermonuclear age, any misjudgment on either side about the intentions of the other could rain more devastation in several hours than has been wrought in all the wars of human history.

Therefore I, as President and Commander-in-Chief, and all of us as Americans, are moving through serious days. I shall bear this responsibility under our Constitution for the next three and one-half years, but I am sure that we all, regardless of our occupations, will do our very best for our country, and for our cause. For all of us want to see our children grow up in a country at peace, and in a world where freedom endures.

I know that sometimes we get impatient, we wish for some immediate action that would end our perils. But I must tell you that there is no quick and easy solution. The Communists control over a billion people, and they recognize that if we should falter, their success would be imminent.

We must look to long days ahead, which if we are courageous and persevering can bring us what we all desire.

In these days and weeks I ask for your help, and your advice. I ask for your suggestions, when you think we could do better.

All of us, I know, love our country, and we shall all do our best to serve it.

In meeting my responsibilities in these coming months as President, I need your good will, and your support - and above all, your prayers.

Agreement Between the President and the Vice President on Procedures In the Event of Presidential Inability
Washington, DC
August 10, 1961

President Kennedy and the Vice President Johnson agreed to adhere to procedures identical to those which former President Eisenhower and Vice President Nixon adopted with regard to any questions of Presidential inability. Those procedures were as follows:

(1) In the event of inability the President would - if possible - so inform the Vice President, and the Vice President would serve as Acting President, exercising the powers and duties of the Office until the inability had ended.

(2) In the event of an inability which would prevent the President from so communicating with the Vice President, the Vice President, after such consultation as seems to him appropriate under the circumstances, would decide upon the devolution of the powers and duties of the Office and would serve as Acting President until the inability had ended.

(3) The President, in either event, would determine when the inability had ended and at that time would resume the full exercise of the powers and duties of the Office.

After consultation with the Attorney General, it is the understanding of the President and the Vice President that these procedures reflect the correct interpretation to be given to Article II, Section I, Clause 5 of the

Constitution. This was also the view of the prior Administration and is supported by the great majority of constitutional scholars.

The relevant constitutional provision is:

> "In Case of the Removal of the President from Office, or of his Death, Resignation, or Inability to discharge the Powers and Duties of the said Office, the same shall devolve on the Vice President, and the Congress may by Law provide for the Case of Removal, Death, Resignation or Inability, both of the President and Vice President, declaring what Officer shall then act as President, and such Officer shall act accordingly, until the Disability be removed, or a President shall be elected."

Under this provision, upon a proper determination of Presidential inability, the Vice President succeeds temporarily to the powers and duties of the Presidency until such time as the President is enabled to act again. Unlike the case of removal, death, or resignation, the Vice President does not permanently become President.

Under the arrangement quoted above, the Vice President agrees to serve as Acting President "after such consultation as seems to him appropriate under the circumstances." There is no provision of the Constitution or of law prescribing any procedure of consultation, but the President and Vice President felt, as a matter of wisdom and sound judgment, that the Vice President would wish to have the support of the Cabinet as to the necessity and desirability of discharging the powers and duties of the Presidency as Acting President as well as legal advice from the Attorney General that the circumstances would, under the Constitution, justify his doing so. The understanding between the President and the Vice President authorizes the Vice President to consult with these officials with a free mind that this is what the President intended in the event of a crisis.

Prior to the Eisenhower-Nixon arrangement, there were no similar understandings of a public nature. For this reason, prior Vice Presidents have hesitated to take any initiative during the period when the President was disabled. Obviously, this is a risk which cannot be taken in these times, and it is for that reason that President Kennedy and Vice President Johnson have agreed to follow the precedent established by the past Administration.

Address To the General Assembly of
the United Nations
New York City
September 25, 1961

We meet in an hour of grief and challenge. Dag Hammarskjold is dead. But the United Nations lives. His tragedy is deep in our hearts, but the task for which he died is at the top of our agenda. A noble servant of peace is gone. But the quest for peace lies before us.

The problem is not the death of one man - the problem is the life of this organization. It will either grow to meet the challenges of our age, or it will be gone with the wind, without influence, without force, without respect. Were we to let it die, to enfeeble its vigor, to cripple its powers, we would condemn our future.

For in the development of this organization rests the only true alternative to war - and war appeals no longer as a rational alternative. Unconditional war can no longer lead to unconditional victory. It can no longer serve to settle disputes. It can no longer concern the great powers alone. For a nuclear disaster, spread by wind and water and fear, could well engulf the great and the small, the rich and the poor, the committed and the uncommitted alike. Mankind must put an end to war - or war will put an end to mankind.

So let us here resolve that Dag Hammarskjold did not live, or die, in vain. Let us call a truce to terror. Let us invoke the blessings of peace. And, as we build an international capacity to keep peace, let us join in dismantling the national capacity to wage war.

This will require new strength and new roles for the United Nations. For disarmament without checks is but a shadow - and a community without law is but a shell. Already the United Nations has become both the measure and the vehicle of man's most generous impulses. Already it has provided - in the Middle East, in Asia, in Africa this year in the Congo - a means of holding man's violence within bounds.

But the great question which confronted this body in 1945 is still before us: whether man's cherished hopes for progress and peace are to be destroyed by terror and disruption, whether the "foul winds of war" can be tamed in time to free the cooling winds of reason, and whether the pledges of our Charter are to be fulfilled or defied - pledges to secure peace, progress, human rights and world law.

In this Hall, there are not three forces, but two. One is composed of those who are trying to build the kind of world described in Articles I and II of the Charter. The other, seeking a far different world, would undermine this organization in the process.

Today of all days our dedication to the Charter must be maintained. It must be strengthened first of all by the selection of an outstanding civil servant to carry forward the responsibilities of the Secretary General - a man endowed with both the wisdom and the power to make meaningful the moral force of the world community. The late Secretary General nurtured and sharpened the United Nations' obligation to act. But he did not invent it. It was there in the Charter. It is still there in the Charter.

However difficult it may be to fill Mr. Hammarskjold's place, it can better be filled by one man rather than by three. Even the three horses of the Troika did not have three drivers, all going indifferent directions. They had only one - and so must the United Nations executive. To install a triumvirate, or any panel, or any rotating authority, in the United Nations administrative offices would replace order with anarchy, action with paralysis, confidence with confusion.

The Secretary General, in a very real sense, is the servant of the General Assembly. Diminish his authority and you diminish the authority of the only body where all nations, regardless of power, are equal and sovereign. Until all the powerful are just, the weak will be secure only in the strength of this Assembly.

Effective and independent executive action is not the same question as balanced representation. In view of the enormous change in membership in this body since its founding, the American delegation will join in any effort for the prompt review and revision of the composition of United Nations bodies.

But to give this organization three drivers - to permit each great power to decide its own case, would entrench the Cold War in the headquarters of peace. Whatever advantages such a plan may hold out to my own country, as one of the great powers, we reject it. For we far prefer world law, in the age of self-determination, to world war, in the age of mass extermination.

Today, every inhabitant of this planet must contemplate the day when this planet may no longer be habitable. Every man, woman and child lives under a nuclear sword of Damocles, hanging by the slenderest of threads, capable of being cut at any moment by accident or miscalculation or by madness. The weapons of war must be abolished before they abolish us.

Men no longer debate whether armaments are a symptom or a cause of tension. The mere existence of modern weapons - ten million times more powerful than any that the world has ever seen, and only minutes away from any target on earth - is a source of horror, and discord and distrust. Men no longer maintain that disarmament must await the settlement of all disputes - for disarmament must be a part of any permanent settlement. And men may no longer pretend that the quest for disarmament is a sign of weakness - for in a spiraling arms race, a nation's security may well be shrinking even as its arms increase.

For 15 years this organization has sought the reduction and destruction of arms. Now that goal is no longer a dream - it is a practical matter of life or death. The risks inherent in disarmament pale in comparison to the risks inherent in an unlimited arms race.

It is in this spirit that the recent Belgrade Conference - recognizing that this is no longer a Soviet problem or an American problem, but a human problem - endorsed a program of "general, complete and strictly an internationally controlled disarmament." It is in this same spirit that we in the United States have labored this year, with a new urgency, and with a new, now statutory agency fully endorsed by the Congress, to find an approach to disarmament which would be so far-reaching yet realistic, so mutually balanced and beneficial, that it could be accepted by every nation. And it is in this spirit that we have presented with the agreement of the Soviet Union -

under the label both nations now accept of "general and complete disarmament" - a new statement of newly-agreed principles for negotiation.

But we are well aware that all issues of principle are not settled, and that principles alone are not enough. It is therefore our intention to challenge the Soviet Union, not to an arms race, but to a peace race - to advance together step by step, stage by stage, until general and complete disarmament has been achieved. We invite them now to go beyond agreement in principle to reach agreement on actual plans.

The program to be presented to this assembly - for general and complete disarmament under effective international control - moves to bridge the gap between those who insist on a gradual approach and those who talk only of the final and total achievement. It would create machinery to keep the peace as it destroys the machinery of war. It would proceed through balanced and safeguarded stages designed to give no state a military advantage over another. It would place the final responsibility for verification and control where it belongs, not with the big powers alone, not with one's adversary or one's self, but in an international organization within the framework of the United Nations. It would assure that indispensable condition of disarmament - true inspection - and apply it in stages proportionate to the stage of disarmament. It would cover delivery systems as well as weapons. It would ultimately halt their production as well as their testing, their transfer as well as their possession. It would achieve, under the eyes of an international disarmament organization, a steady reduction in force, both nuclear and conventional, until it has abolished all armies and all weapons except those needed for internal order and a new United Nations Peace Force. And it starts that process now, today, even as the talks begin.

In short, general and complete disarmament must no longer be a slogan, used to resist the first steps. It is no longer to be a goal without means of achieving it, without means of verifying its progress, without means of keeping the peace. It is now a realistic plan, and a test - a test of those only willing to talk and a test of those willing to act.

Such a plan would not bring a world free from conflict and greed - but it would bring a world free from the terrors of mass destruction. It would not usher in the era of the super state - but it would usher in an era in which no state could annihilate or be annihilated by another.

In 1945, this Nation proposed the Baruch Plan to internationalize the atom before other nations even possessed the bomb or demilitarized their troops. We proposed with our allies the Disarmament Plan of 1951 while still at war in Korea. And we make our proposals today, while building up our defenses over Berlin, not because we are inconsistent or insincere or intimidated, but because we know the rights of free men will prevail - because while we are compelled against our will to rearm, we look confidently beyond Berlin to the kind of disarmed world we all prefer.

I therefore propose, on the basis of this Plan, that disarmament negotiations resume promptly, and continue without interruption until an entire program for general and complete disarmament has not only been agreed but has been actually achieved.

The logical place to begin is a treaty assuring the end of nuclear tests of all kinds, in every environment, under workable controls.   The United States and the United Kingdom have proposed such a treaty that is both reasonable, effective and ready for signature. We are still prepared to sign that treaty today.

We also proposed a mutual ban on atmospheric testing, without inspection or controls, in order to save the human race from the poison of radioactive fallout. We regret that that offer has not been accepted.

For 15 years we have sought to make the atom an instrument of peaceful growth rather than of war. But for 15 years our concessions have been matched by obstruction, our patience by intransigence. And the pleas of mankind for peace have met with disregard.

Finally, as the explosions of others beclouded the skies, my country was left with no alternative but to act in the interests of its own and the free world's security. We cannot endanger that security by refraining from testing while others improve their arsenals. Nor can we endanger it by another long, uninspected ban on testing. For three years we accepted those risks in our open society while seeking agreement on inspection. But this year, while we were negotiating in good faith in Geneva, others were secretly preparing new experiments in destruction.

Our tests are not polluting the atmosphere. Our deterrent weapons are guarded against accidental explosion or use. Our doctors and scientists stand ready to help any nation measure and meet the hazards to health which inevitably result from the tests in the atmosphere.

But to halt the spread of these terrible weapons, to halt the contamination of the air, to halt the spiralling nuclear arms race, we remain ready to seek new avenues of agreement, our new Disarmament Program thus includes the following proposals:

First, signing the test-ban treaty by all nations. This can be done now. Test ban negotiations need not and should not await general disarmament.

Second, stopping the production of fissionable materials for use in weapons, and preventing their transfer to any nation now lacking in nuclear weapons.

Third, prohibiting the transfer of control over nuclear weapons to states that do not own them.

Fourth, keeping nuclear weapons from seeding new battlegrounds in outer space.

Fifth, gradually destroying existing nuclear weapons and converting their materials to peaceful uses; and

Finally, halting the unlimited testing and production of strategic nuclear delivery vehicles, and gradually destroying them as well.

To destroy arms, however, is not enough. We must create even as we destroy - creating worldwide law and law enforcement as we outlaw worldwide war and weapons. In the world we seek, the United Nations Emergency Forces which have been hastily assembled, uncertainly supplied, and inadequately financed, will never be enough.

Therefore, the United States recommends that all member nations earmark special peacekeeping units in their armed forces - to be on call of the United Nations, to be specially trained and quickly available, and with advance provision for financial and logistic support.

In addition, the American delegation will suggest a series of steps to improve the United Nations' machinery for the peaceful settlement of disputes - for on-the-spot fact - finding, mediation and adjudication for extending the rule of international law. For peace is not solely a matter of military or technical problems - it is primarily a problem of politics and people. And unless man can match his strides in weaponry and technology with equal strides, in social and political development, our great strength, like that of the dinosaur, will become incapable of proper control - and like the dinosaur vanish from the earth.

As we extend the rule of law on earth, so must we also extend it to man's new domain - outer space.

All of us salute the brave cosmonauts of the Soviet Union. The new horizons of outer space must not be driven by the old bitter concepts of imperialism and sovereign claims. The cold reaches of the universe must not become the new arena of an even colder war.

To this end, we shall urge proposals extending the United Nations Charter to the limits of man's exploration in the universe, reserving outer space for peaceful use, prohibiting weapons of mass destruction in space or on celestial bodies, and opening the mysteries and benefits of space to every nation. We shall propose further cooperative efforts between all nations in weather prediction and eventually in weather control. We shall propose, finally, a global system of communications satellites linking the whole world in telegraph and telephone and radio and television. The day need not be far away when such a system will televise the proceedings of this body to every corner of the world for the benefit of peace.

But the mysteries of outer space must not divert our eyes or our energies from the harsh realities that face our fellow men. Political sovereignty is but a mockery without the means of meeting poverty and illiteracy and disease. Self-determination is but a slogan if the future holds no hope.

That is why my Nation, which has freely shared its capital and its technology to help others help themselves, now proposes officially designating this decade of the 1960's as the United Nations Decade of Development. Under the framework of that Resolution, the United Nations' existing efforts in promoting economic growth can be expanded and coordinated. Regional surveys and training institutes can now pool the talents of many. New research, technical assistance and pilot projects can unlock the wealth of less developed lands and untapped waters. And development can become a cooperative and not a competitive enterprise - to enable all nations, however diverse in their systems and beliefs, to become in fact as well as in law free and equal nations.

My country favors a world of free and equal states. We agree with those who say that colonialism is a key issue in this Assembly. But let the full facts of that issue be discussed in full.

On the one hand is the fact that, since the close of World War II, a worldwide declaration of independence has transformed nearly 1 billion people and 9 million square miles into 42 free and independent states. Less than 2 percent of the world's population now lives in "dependent" territories.

I do not ignore the remaining problems of traditional colonialism which still confront this body. Those problems will be solved, with patience, good will, and determination. Within the limits of our responsibility in such matters, my Country intends to be a participant and not merely an observer, in the peaceful, expeditious movement of nations from the status of colonies to the partnership of equals. That continuing tide of self-determination, which runs so strong, has our sympathy and our support.

But colonialism in its harshest forms is not only the exploitation of new nations by old, of dark skins by light, or the subjugation of the poor by the rich. My Nation was once a colony, and we know what colonialism means; the exploitation and subjugation of the weak by the powerful, of the many by the few, of the governed who have given no consent to be governed, whatever their continent, their class, or their color.

And that is why there is no ignoring the fact that the tide of self-determination has not reached the Communist empire where a population far larger than that officially termed "dependent" lives under governments installed by foreign troops instead of free institutions - under a system which knows only one party and one belief - which suppresses free debate, and free elections, and free newspapers, and free books and free trade unions - and which builds a wall to keep truth a stranger and its own citizens prisoners. Let us debate colonialism in full - and apply the principle of free choice and the practice of free plebiscites in every corner of the globe.

Finally, as President of the United States, I consider it my duty to report to this Assembly on two threats to the peace which are not on your crowded agenda, but which causes us, and most of you, the deepest concern.

The first threat on which I wish to report is widely misunderstood: the smoldering coals of war in Southeast Asia. South Viet Nam is already under attack - sometimes by a single assassin, sometimes by a band of guerrillas, recently by full battalions. The peaceful borders of Burma, Cambodia, and India have been repeatedly violated. And the peaceful people of Laos are in danger of losing the independence they gained not so long ago.

No one can call these "wars of liberation." For these are free countries living under their own governments. Nor are these aggressions any less real because men are knifed in their homes and not shot in the fields of battle.

The very simple question confronting the world community is whether measures can be devised to protect the small and the weak from such tactics. For if they are successful in Laos and South Viet Nam, the gates will be opened wide.

The United States seeks for itself no base, no territory, no special position in this area of any kind. We support a truly neutral and independent Laos, its people free from outside interference, living at peace with themselves and with their neighbors, assured that their territory will not be used for attacks on others, and under a government comparable (as Mr. Khrushchev and I agreed at Vienna) to Cambodia and Burma.

But now the negotiations over Laos are reaching a crucial stage. The ceasefire is at best precarious. The rainy season is coming to an end. Laotian territory is being used to infiltrate South Viet Nam. The world community must recognize - and all those who are involved - that this potent threat to Laotian peace and freedom is indivisible from all other threats to their own.

Secondly, I wish to report to you on the crisis over Germany and Berlin. This is not the time or the place for immoderate tones, but the world community is entitled to know the very simple issues as we see them. If there is a crisis it is because an existing peace is under threat, because an existing island of free people is under pressure, because solemn agreements are being treated with indifference. Established international rights arc being threatened with unilateral usurpation. Peaceful circulation has been interrupted by barbed wire and concrete blocks.

One recalls the order of the Czar in Pushkin's "Boris Godunov": "Take steps at this very hour that our frontiers be fenced in by barriers. . . . That not a single soul pass o'er the border, that not a hare be able to run or a crow to fly."

It is absurd to allege that we are threatening a war merely to prevent the Soviet Union and East Germany from signing a so-called "treaty" of peace. The Western Allies are not concerned with any paper arrangement the Soviets may wish to make with a regime of their own creation, on territory occupied by their own troops and governed by their own agents. No such action can affect either our rights or our responsibilities.

If there is a dangerous crisis in Berlin - and there is - it is because of threats against the vital interests and the deep commitments of the Western Powers, and the freedom of West Berlin. We cannot yield these interests. We cannot fail these commitments. We cannot surrender the freedom of these people for whom we are responsible. A "peace treaty" which carried with it the provisions which destroy the peace would be a fraud. A "free city" which was not genuinely free would suffocate freedom and would be an infamy.

For a city or a people to be truly free, they must have the secure right, without economic, political or police pressure, to make their own choice and to live their own lives. And as I have said before, if anyone doubts the extent to which our presence is desired by the people of West Berlin, we are ready to have that question submitted to a free vote in all Berlin and, if possible, among all the German people.

The elementary fact about this crisis is that it is unnecessary. The elementary tools for a peaceful settlement are to be found in the Charter. Under its law, agreements are to be kept, unless changed by all those who made them. Established rights are to be respected. The political disposition of peoples should rest upon their own wishes, freely expressed in plebiscites or free elections. If there are legal problems, they can be solved by legal means. If there is a threat of force, it must be rejected. If there is desire for change, it must be a subject for negotiation and if there is negotiation, it must be rooted in mutual respect and concern for the rights of others.

The Western Powers have calmly resolved to defend, by whatever means are forced upon them, their obligations and their access to the free citizens of West Berlin and the self-determination of those citizens. This generation learned from bitter experience that either brandishing or yielding to threats can only lead to war. But firmness and reason can lead to the kind of peaceful solution in which my country profoundly believes.

We are committed to no rigid formula. We see no perfect solution. We recognize that troops and tanks can, for a time, keep a nation divided against its will, however unwise that policy may seem to us. But we believe a peaceful agreement is possible which protects the freedom of West Berlin and allied presence and access, while recognizing the historic and legitimate interests of others in assuring European security.

The possibilities of negotiation are now being explored; it is too early to report what the prospects may be. For our part, we would be glad to report at the appropriate time that a solution has been found. For there is no need for a crisis over Berlin, threatening the peace - and if those who created this crisis desire peace, there will be peace and freedom in Berlin.

The events and decisions of the next ten months may well decide the fate of man for the next ten thousand years. There will be no avoiding those events. There will be no appeal from these decisions. And we in this hall shall be remembered either as part of the generation that turned this planet into a flaming funeral pyre or the generation that met its vow "to save succeeding generations from the scourge of war."

In the endeavor to meet that vow, I pledge you every effort this Nation possesses. I pledge you that we shall neither commit nor provoke aggression, that we shall neither flee nor invoke the threat of force, that we shall never negotiate out of fear, we shall never fear to negotiate.

Terror is not a new weapon. Throughout history it has been used by those who could not prevail, either by persuasion or example. But inevitably they fail, either because men are not afraid to die for a life worth living, or because the terrorists themselves came to realize that free men cannot be frightened by threats, and that aggression would meet its own response. And it is in the light of that history that every nation today should know, be he friend or foe, that the United States has both the will and the weapons to join free men in standing up to their responsibilities.

But I come here today to look across this world of threats to a world of peace. In that search we cannot expect any final triumph - for new problems will always arise. We cannot expect that all nations will adopt like systems - for conformity is the jailor of freedom, and the enemy of growth. Nor can we expect to reach our goal by contrivance, by fiat or even by the wishes of all.

But however close we sometimes seem to that dark and final abyss, let no man of peace and freedom despair. For he does not stand alone. If we all can persevere, if we can in every land and office look beyond our own shores and ambitions, then surely the age will dawn in which the strong are just and the weak secure and the peace preserved.

Ladies and gentlemen of this Assembly, the decision is ours. Never have the nations of the world had so much to lose, or so much to gain. Together we shall save our planet, or together we shall perish in its flames. Save it we can - and save it we must - and then shall we earn the eternal thanks of mankind and, as peacemakers, the eternal blessing of God.

Creation of the President's Commission on The Status of Women
Washington, DC
December 14, 1961

Forty-one years have passed since the first national election in which women were permitted to vote.

As was foreseen by the early leaders, women have brought into public affairs great sensitivity to human need and opposition to selfish and corrupt purposes. These political contributions and the manifold activities of women in American communities are the outgrowth of a long tradition of pioneering by American women. They stand as an encouraging example to countries in which women are only now achieving equal political and social status.

Yet we do well not to be complacent about past progress. Undoubtedly the ever-advancing frontier in our country helped to break down attitudes carried over from feudal days. But we have by no means done enough to strengthen family life and at the same time encourage women to make their full contribution as citizens.

If our Nation is to be successful in the critical period ahead, we must rely upon the skills and devotion of all our people. In every time of crisis, women have served our country in difficult and hazardous ways. They will do so now, in the home and at work. We naturally deplore those economic conditions which require women to work unless they desire to do so, and the programs of our Administration are designed to improve family incomes so that women can make their own decisions in this area. Women should not be considered a marginal group to be employed periodically only to be denied opportunity to satisfy their needs and aspirations when unemployment rises or a war ends.

Women have basic rights which should be respected and fostered as part of our Nation's commitment to human dignity, freedom, and democracy.

It is appropriate at this time, when we are observing Human Rights Week, to set forth before the world the story of women's progress in a free, democratic society, to review recent accomplishments, and to acknowledge frankly the further steps that must be taken.

This is a task for the entire Nation.

To help with specific analysis and recommendations, I am today, upon the recommendation of the Secretary of Labor, establishing The President's Commission on the Status of Women. I am directing appropriate Federal departments and agencies to cooperate with the Commission in developing plans for advancing the full partnership of men and women in our national life.

The Commission is to complete its work and publish a report by October 1, 1963. I am asking that it consider the following broad range of topics, making recommendations on those where constructive action is needed:

1. Employment policies and practices of the Federal Government.

2. Employment policies and practices, including those on wages, under Federal contracts.

3. Effects of Federal social insurance programs and tax laws on the net earnings and other income of women.

4. Appraisal of Federal and State labor laws dealing with such matters as hours, night work, and wages, to determine whether they are accomplishing the purposes for which they were established and whether they need to be adapted to changing technological, economic, and social conditions.

5. Differences in legal treatment of men and women in regard to political and civil rights, property rights, and family relations.

6. New and expanded services that may be required for women as wives, mothers, and workers, including education, counseling, training, home services, and arrangements for care of children during the working day.

In addition to its own small staff, the Commission will be assisted by the U.S. Department of Labor, the Civil Service Commission, and other appropriate Federal agencies. It will seek the cooperation of a wide variety of individuals and civic groups, especially national organizations which have already done so much to advance women's welfare; it will request information from the States on their laws and experience; it will utilize subcommittees to develop proposals in specialized fields.

It is my hope that the Commission's Report will indicate what remains to be done to demolish prejudices and outmoded customs which act as barriers to the full partnership of women in our democracy. The Commission will welcome recommendations from all groups on this crucial matter. Progress will require the cooperation of the whole community.

Many of the old legal disabilities have been swept away. Some still remain. But more than their removal is required. Attention must be given to opening up greater employment opportunities for women as well as removing remaining discriminations against them.

The great majority of women now seek gainful employment at some period of their lives. The community should make it possible for them to make the best use of their talents and to function constructively, both through legislation and through necessary supportive services by private or public agencies.

Women are entitled to equality of opportunity for employment in government and in industry. But a mere statement supporting equality of opportunity must be implemented by affirmative steps to see that the doors are really open for training, selection, advancement, and equal pay.

I believe that Federal employment practices should be a showcase of the feasibility and value of combining genuine equality of opportunity on the basis of merit with efficient service to the public.

It is my firm intent that the Federal career service be maintained in every respect without discrimination and with equal opportunity for employment and advancement. I have, therefore, requested the Chairman of the Civil Service Commission to review pertinent personnel policies and practices affecting the employment of women and to work with the various departments and agencies to assure that selection for any career position is hereafter made solely on the basis of individual merit and fitness, without regard to sex.

The State of the Union
Washington, DC
January 11, 1962

This week we begin anew our joint and separate efforts to build the American future. But, sadly, we build without a man who linked a long past with the present and looked strongly to the future. "Mister Sam" Rayburn is gone. Neither this House nor the Nation is the same without him.

Members of the Congress, the Constitution makes us not rivals for power but partners for progress. We are all trustees for the American people, custodians of the American heritage. It is my task to *report* the State of the Union - to *improve* it is the task of us all.

In the past year, I have travelled not only across our own land but to other lands - to the North and the South, and across the seas. And I have found - as I am sure you have, in your travels - that people everywhere, in spite of occasional disappointments, look to us - not to our wealth or power, but to the splendor of our ideals. For our Nation is commissioned by history to be either an observer of freedom's failure or the cause of its success. Our overriding obligation in the months ahead is to fulfill the world's hopes by fulfilling our own faith.

That task must begin at home. For if we cannot fulfill our own ideals here, we cannot expect others to accept them. And when the youngest child alive today has grown to the cares of manhood, our position in the world will be determined first of all by what provisions we make today - for his education, his health, and his opportunities for a good home and a good job and a good life.

At home, we began the year in the valley of recession - we completed it on the high road of recovery and growth. With the help of new congressionally approved or administratively increased stimulants to our economy, the number of major surplus labor areas has declined from 101 to 60; nonagricultural employment has increased by more than a million jobs; and the average factory work-week has risen to well over 40 hours. At year's end the economy which Mr. Khrushchev once called a "stumbling horse" was racing to new records in consumer spending, labor income, and industrial production.

We are gratified - but we are not satisfied. Too many unemployed are still looking for the blessings of prosperity. As those who leave our schools and farms demand new jobs, automation takes old jobs away. To expand our growth and job opportunities, I urge on the Congress three measures:

First, the Manpower Training and Development Act, to stop the waste of able-bodied men and women who want to work, but whose only skill has been replaced by a machine, or moved with a mill, or shut down with a mine;

Second, the Youth Employment Opportunities Act, to help train and place not only the one million young Americans who are both out of school and out of work, but the twenty-six million young Americans entering the labor market in this decade; and

Third, the 8 percent tax credit for investment in machinery and equipment, which, combined with planned revisions of depreciation allowances, will spur our modernization, our growth, and our ability to compete abroad.

Moreover - pleasant as it may be to bask in the warmth of recovery - let us not forget that we have suffered three recessions in the last 7 years. The time to repair the roof is when the sun is shining by filling three basic gaps in our anti-recession protection. We need:

First, Presidential standby authority, subject to congressional veto, to adjust personal income tax rates downward within a specified range and time, to slow down an economic decline before it has dragged us all down;

Second, Presidential standby authority, upon a given rise in the rate of unemployment, to accelerate Federal and federally-aided capital improvement programs; and

Third, a permanent strengthening of our unemployment compensation system - to maintain for our fellow citizens searching for a job who cannot find it, their purchasing power and their living standards without constant resort - as we have seen in recent years by the Congress and the administrations - to temporary supplements.

If we enact this six part program, we can show the whole world that a free economy need not be an unstable economy that a free system need not leave men unemployed and that a free society is not only the most productive but the most stable form of organization yet fashioned by man.

But recession is only one enemy of a free economy - inflation is another. Last year, 1961, despite rising production and demand, consumer prices held almost steady - and wholesale prices declined. This is the best record of overall price stability of any comparable period of recovery since the end of World War II.

Inflation too often follows in the shadow of growth - while price stability is made easy by stagnation or controls. But we mean to maintain both stability and growth in a climate of freedom.

Our first line of defense against inflation is the good sense and public spirit of business and labor - keeping their total increases in wages and profits in step with productivity. There is no single statistical test to guide each company and each union. But I strongly urge them - for their country's interest, and for their own - to apply the test of the public interest to these transactions.

Within this same framework of growth and wage-price stability:

This administration has helped keep our economy competitive by widening the access of small business to credit and Government contracts, and by stepping up the drive against monopoly, price-fixing, and racketeering;

We will submit a Federal Pay Reform bill aimed at giving our classified, postal, and other employees new pay scales more comparable to those of private industry;

We are holding the fiscal 1962 budget deficit far below the level incurred after the last recession in 1958; and, finally, I am submitting for fiscal 1963 a balanced Federal Budget.

This is a joint responsibility, requiring Congressional cooperation on appropriations, and on three sources of income in particular:

First, an increase in postal rates, to end the postal deficit;

Secondly, passage of the tax reforms previously urged, to remove unwarranted tax preferences, and to apply to dividends and to interest the same withholding requirements we have long applied to wages; and

Third, extension of the present excise and corporation tax rates, except for those changes - which will be recommended in a message - affecting transportation.

But a stronger nation and economy require more than a balanced Budget. They require progress in those programs that spur our growth and fortify our strength.

A strong America depends on its cities - America's glory, and sometimes America's shame. To substitute sunlight for congestion and progress for decay, we have stepped up existing urban renewal and housing programs, and launched new ones - redoubled the attack on water pollution - speeded aid to airports, hospitals, highways, and our declining mass transit systems - and secured new weapons to combat organized crime, racketeering, and youth delinquency, assisted by the coordinated and hard-hitting efforts of our investigative services: the FBI, the Internal Revenue, the Bureau of Narcotics, and many others. We shall need further anti-crime, mass transit, and transportation legislation - and new tools to fight air pollution. And with all this effort underway, both equity and common sense require that our nation's urban areas - containing three-fourths of our population - sit as equals at the Cabinet table. I urge a new Department of Urban Affairs and Housing.

A strong America also depends on its farms and natural resources. American farmers took heart in 1961 - from a billion dollar rise in farm income - and from a hopeful start on reducing the farm surpluses. But we are still operating under a patchwork accumulation of old laws, which cost us $1 billion a year in CCC carrying charges alone, yet fail to halt rural poverty or boost farm earnings.

Our task is to master and turn to fully fruitful ends the magnificent productivity of our farms and farmers. The revolution on our own countryside stands in the sharpest contrast to the repeated farm failures of the Communist nations and is a source of pride to us all. Since 1950 our agricultural output per man-hour has actually doubled! Without new, realistic measures, it will someday swamp our farmers and our taxpayers in a national scandal or a farm depression.

I will, therefore, submit to the Congress a new comprehensive farm program - tailored to fit the use of our land and the supplies of each crop to the long range needs of the sixties - and designed to prevent chaos in the sixties with a program of common sense.

We also need for the sixties - if we are to bequeath our full national estate to our heirs - a new long range conservation and recreation program - expansion of our superb national parks and forests - preservation of our authentic wilderness areas - new starts on water and power projects as our population steadily increases - and expanded REA generation and transmission loans.

But America stands for progress in human rights as well as economic affairs, and a strong America requires the assurance of full and equal rights to all its citizens, of any race or of any color. This administration has shown as never before how much could be done through the full use of Executive powers - through the enforcement of laws already passed by the Congress - through persuasion, negotiation, and litigation, to secure the constitutional rights of all: the right to vote, the right to travel without hindrance across State lines, and the right to free public education.

I issued last March a comprehensive order to guarantee the right to equal employment opportunity in all Federal agencies and contractors. The Vice President's Committee thus created has done much, including the voluntary "Plans for Progress" which, in all sections of the country, are achieving a quiet but striking success in opening up to all races new professional, supervisory, and other job opportunities.

But there is much more to be done - by the Executive, by the courts, and by the Congress. Among the bills now pending before you, on which the executive departments will comment in detail, are appropriate methods of strengthening these basic rights which have our full support. The right to vote, for example, should no longer be denied through such arbitrary devices on a local level, sometimes abused, such as literacy tests and poll taxes. As we approach the 100th anniversary, next January, of the Emancipation Proclamation, let the acts of every branch of the Government - and every citizen - portray that "righteousness does not exalt a nation."

Finally, a strong America cannot neglect the aspirations of its citizens - the welfare of the needy, the health care of the elderly, the education of the young. For we are not developing the Nation's wealth for its own sake. Wealth is the means - and people are the ends. All our material riches will avail us little if we do not use them to expand the opportunities of our people.

Last year, we improved the diet of needy people - provided more hot lunches and fresh milk to school children - built more college dormitories - and, for the elderly, expanded private housing, nursing homes, health services, and social security. But we have just begun.

To help those least fortunate of all, I am recommending a new public welfare program, stressing services instead of support, rehabilitation instead of relief, and training for useful work instead of prolonged dependency.

To relieve the critical shortage of doctors and dentists - and this is a matter which should concern us all - and expand research, I urge action to aid medical and dental colleges and scholarships and to establish new National Institutes of Health.

To take advantage of modern vaccination achievements, I am proposing a mass immunization program, aimed at the virtual elimination of such ancient enemies of our children as polio, diphtheria, whooping cough, and tetanus.

To protect our consumers from the careless and the unscrupulous, I shall recommend improvements in the

Food and Drug laws - strengthening inspection and standards, halting unsafe and worthless products, preventing misleading labels, and cracking down on the illicit sale of habit-forming drugs.

But in matters of health, no piece of unfinished business is more important or more urgent than the enactment under the social security system of health insurance for the aged.

For our older citizens have longer and more frequent illnesses, higher hospital and medical bills and too little income to pay them. Private health insurance helps very few - for its cost is high and its coverage limited. Public welfare cannot help those too proud to seek relief but hard-pressed to pay their own bills. Nor can their children or grandchildren always sacrifice their own health budgets to meet this constant drain.

Social security has long helped to meet the hardships of retirement, death, and disability. I now urge that its coverage be extended without further delay to provide health insurance for the elderly.

Equally important to our strength is the quality of our education. Eight million adult Americans are classified as functionally illiterate. This is a disturbing figure - reflected in Selective Service rejection rates - reflected in welfare rolls and crime rates. And I shall recommend plans for a massive attack to end this adult illiteracy.

I shall also recommend bills to improve educational quality, to stimulate the arts, and, at the college level, to provide Federal loans for the construction of academic facilities and federally financed scholarships.

If this Nation is to grow in wisdom and strength, then every able high school graduate should have the opportunity to develop his talents. Yet nearly half lack either the funds or the facilities to attend college. Enrollments are going to double in our colleges in the short space of 10 years. The annual cost per student is skyrocketing to astronomical levels - now averaging $1,650 a year, although almost half of our families earn less than $5,000. They cannot afford such costs - but this Nation cannot afford to maintain its military power and neglect its brainpower.

But excellence in education must begin at the elementary level. I sent to the Congress last year a proposal for Federal aid to public school construction and teachers' salaries. I believe that bill, which passed the Senate and received House Committee approval, offered the minimum amount required by our needs and - in terms of across-the-board aid - the maximum scope permitted by our Constitution. I therefore see no reason to weaken or withdraw that bill: and I urge its passage at this session.

"Civilization," said H.G. Wells, "is a race between education and catastrophe." It is up to you in this Congress to determine the winner of that race.

These are not unrelated measures addressed to specific gaps or grievances in our national life. They are the pattern of our intentions and the foundation of our hopes. "I believe in democracy," said Woodrow Wilson, "because it releases the energy of every human being." The dynamic of democracy is the power and the purpose of the individual, and the policy of this administration is to give to the individual the opportunity to realize his own highest possibilities.

Our program is to open to all the opportunity for steady and productive employment, to remove from all the handicap of arbitrary or irrational exclusion, to offer to all the facilities for education and health and welfare, to make society the servant of the individual and the individual the source of progress, and thus to realize for all the full promise of American life.

All of these efforts at home give meaning to our efforts abroad. Since the close of the Second World War, a global civil war has divided and tormented mankind. But it is not our military might, or our higher standard of living, that has most distinguished us from our adversaries. It is our belief that the state is the servant of the citizen and not his master.

This basic clash of ideas and wills is but one of the forces reshaping our globe - swept as it is by the tides of hope and fear, by crises in the headlines today that become mere footnotes tomorrow. Both the successes and the setbacks of the past year remain on our agenda of unfinished business. For every apparent blessing contains the seeds of danger - every area of trouble gives out a ray of hope - and the one unchangeable certainty is that nothing is certain or unchangeable.

Yet our basic goal remains the same: a peaceful world community of free and independent states - free to choose their own future and their own system, so long as it does not threaten the freedom of others.

Some may choose forms and ways that we would not choose for ourselves - but it is not for us that they are choosing. We can welcome diversity - the Communists cannot. For we offer a world of choice - they offer the world of coercion. And the way of the past shows clearly that freedom, not coercion, is the wave of the future. At times our goal has been obscured by crisis or endangered by conflict - but it draws sustenance from five basic sources of strength:

> the moral and physical strength of the United States;

> the united strength of the Atlantic Community;

> the regional strength of our Hemispheric relations;

> the creative strength of our efforts in the new and developing nations; and

> the peacekeeping strength of the United Nations.

Our moral and physical strength begins at home as already discussed. But it includes our military strength as well. So long as fanaticism and fear brood over the affairs of men, we must arm to deter others from aggression.

In the past 12 months our military posture has steadily improved. We increased the previous defense budget by 15 percent - not in the expectation of war but for the preservation of peace. We more than doubled our acquisition rate of Polaris submarines - we doubled the production capacity for Minuteman missiles - and increased by 50 percent the number of manned bombers standing ready on a 15 minute alert. This year the combined force levels planned under our new Defense budget - including nearly three hundred additional Polaris and Minuteman missiles - have been precisely calculated to insure the continuing strength of our nuclear deterrent.

But our strength may be tested at many levels. We intend to have at all times the capacity to resist non-nuclear or limited attacks - as a complement to our nuclear capacity, not as a substitute. We have rejected any all-or-nothing posture which would leave no choice but inglorious retreat or unlimited retaliation.

Thus we have doubled the number of ready combat divisions in the Army's strategic reserve - increased our troops in Europe - built up the Marines - added new sealift and airlift capacity - modernized our weapons and ammunition expanded our anti-guerrilla forces - and increased the active fleet by more than 70 vessels and our tactical air forces by nearly a dozen wings.

Because we needed to reach this higher long-term level of readiness more quickly, 155,000 members of the Reserve and National Guard were activated under the Act of this Congress. Some disruptions and distress were inevitable. But the overwhelming majority bear their burdens - and their Nation's burdens - with admirable and traditional devotion.

In the coming year, our reserve programs will be revised - two Army Divisions will, I hope, replace those Guard Divisions on duty - and substantial other increases will boost our Air Force fighter units, the procurement of equipment, and our continental defense and warning efforts. The Nation's first serious civil defense shelter program is under way, identifying, marking, and stocking 50 million spaces; and I urge your approval of Federal incentives for the construction of public fallout shelters in schools and hospitals and similar centers.

But arms alone are not enough to keep the peace - it must be kept by men. Our instrument and our hope is the United Nations - and I see little merit in the impatience of those who would abandon this imperfect world instrument because they dislike our imperfect world. For the troubles of a world organization merely reflect the troubles of the world itself. And if the organization is weakened, these troubles can only increase. We may not always agree with every detailed action taken by every officer of the United Nations, or with every voting majority. But as an institution, it should have in the future, as it has had in the past since its inception, no stronger or more faithful member than the United States of America.

In 1961 the peacekeeping strength of the United Nations was reinforced. And those who preferred or predicted its demise, envisioning a troika in the seat of Hammarskjold - or Red China inside the Assembly - have seen instead a new vigor, under a new Secretary General and a fully independent Secretariat. In making plans for a new forum and principles on disarmament - for peacekeeping in outer space - for a decade of development effort - the U.N. fulfilled its Charter's lofty aim.

Eighteen months ago the tangled and turbulent Congo presented the U.N. with its gravest challenge. The prospect was one of chaos - or certain big-power confrontation, with all of its hazards and all of its risks, to us and to others. Today the hopes have improved for peaceful conciliation within a united Congo. This is the objective of our policy in this important area.

No policeman is universally popular - particularly when he uses his stick to restore law and order on his beat. Those members who are willing to contribute their votes and their views - but very little else - have created a serious deficit by refusing to pay their share of special U.N. assessments. Yet they do pay their annual assessments to retain their votes - and a new U.N. Bond issue, financing special operations for the next 18 months, is to be repaid with interest from these regular assessments. This is clearly in our interest. It will not only keep the U.N. solvent, but require all voting members to pay their fair share of its activities. Our share of special operations has long been much higher than our share of the annual assessment - and the bond issue will in effect reduce our disproportionate obligation, and for these reasons, I am urging Congress to approve our participation.

With the approval of this Congress, we have undertaken in the past year a great new effort in outer space. Our aim is not simply to be first on the moon, any more than Charles Lindbergh's real aim was to be the first to Paris. His aim was to develop the techniques of our own country and other countries in the field of air and the atmosphere, and our objective in making this effort, which we hope will place one of our citizens on the moon, is to develop in a new frontier of science, commerce and cooperation, the position of the United States and the Free World.

This Nation belongs among the first to explore it, and among the first - if not the first - we shall be. We are offering our know-how and our cooperation to the United

Nations. Our satellites will soon be providing other
nations with improved weather observations. And I shall
soon send to the Congress a measure to govern the
financing and operation of an International
Communications Satellite system in a manner consistent
with the public interest and our foreign policy.

But peace in space will help us naught once peace on
earth is gone. World order will be secured only when the
whole world has laid down these weapons which seem to
offer us present security but threaten the future survival
of the human race. That armistice day seems very far
away. The vast resources of this planet are being devoted
more and more to the means of destroying, instead of
enriching, human life.

But the world was not meant to be a prison in which man
awaits his execution. Nor has mankind survived the tests
and trials of thousands of years to surrender everything -
including its existence - now. This Nation has the will
and the faith to make a supreme effort to break the log
jam on disarmament and nuclear tests and we will persist
until we prevail, until the rule of law has replaced the
ever dangerous use of force.

I turn now to a prospect of great promise: our
Hemispheric relations. The Alliance for Progress is being
rapidly transformed from proposal to program. Last
month in Latin America I saw for myself the quickening
of hope, the revival of confidence, the new trust in our
country - among workers and farmers as well as
diplomats. We have pledged our help in speeding their
economic, educational, and social progress. The Latin
American Republics have in turn pledged a new and
strenuous effort of self-help and self-reform.

To support this historic undertaking, I am proposing - under the authority contained in the bills of the last session of the Congress - a special long-term Alliance for Progress fund of $3 billion. Combined with our Food for Peace, Export-Import Bank, and other resources, this will provide more that $1 billion a year in new support for the Alliance. In addition, we have increased twelvefold our Spanish and Portuguese language broadcasting in Latin America, and improved Hemispheric trade and defense. And while the blight of communism has been increasingly exposed and isolated in the Americas, liberty has scored a gain. The people of the Dominican Republic, with our firm encouragement and help, and those of our sister Republics of this Hemisphere are safely passing through the treacherous course from dictatorship through disorder towards democracy.

Our efforts to help other new or developing nations, and to strengthen their stand for freedom, have also made progress. A newly unified Agency for International Development is reorienting our foreign assistance to emphasize long-term development loans instead of grants, more economic aid instead of military, individual plans to meet the individual needs of the nations, and new standards on what they must do to marshal their own resources.

A newly conceived Peace Corps is winning friends and helping people in fourteen countries - supplying trained and dedicated young men and women, to give these new nations a hand in building a society, and a glimpse of the best that is in our country. If there is a problem here, it is that we cannot supply the spontaneous and mounting demand.

A newly-expanded Food for Peace Program is feeding the hungry of many lands with the abundance of our productive farms - providing lunches for children in school, wages for economic development, relief for the victims of flood and famine, and a better diet for millions whose daily bread is their chief concern.

These programs help people; and, by helping people, they help freedom. The views of their governments may sometimes be very different from ours - but events in Africa, the Middle East, and Eastern Europe teach us never to write off any nation as lost to the Communists. That is the lesson of our time. We support the independence of those newer or weaker states whose history, geography, economy or lack of power impels them to remain outside "entangling alliances" - as we did for more than a century. For the independence of nations is a bar to the Communists' "grand design" it is the basis of our own.

In the past year, for example, we have urged a neutral and independent Laos - regained there a common policy with our major allies - and insisted that a ceasefire precede negotiations. While a workable formula for supervising its independence is still to be achieved, both the spread of war which might have involved this country also - and a Communist occupation have thus far been prevented.

A satisfactory settlement in Laos would also help to achieve and safeguard the peace in Viet Nam - where the foe is increasing his tactics of terror - where our own efforts have been stepped up - and where the local government has initiated new programs and reforms to broaden the base of resistance. The systematic aggression now bleeding that country is not a "war of liberation" -

for Viet Nam is already free. It is a war of attempted subjugation - and it will be resisted.

Finally, the united strength of the Atlantic Community has flourished in the last year under severe tests. NATO has increased both the number and the readiness of its air, ground, and naval units - both its nuclear and non-nuclear capabilities. Even greater efforts by all its members are still required. Nevertheless our unity of purpose and will has been, I believe, immeasurably strengthened.

The threat to the brave city of Berlin remains. In these last 6 months the Allies have made it unmistakably clear that our presence in Berlin, our free access thereto, and the freedom of two million West Berliners would not be surrendered either to force or through appeasement - and to maintain those rights and obligations, we are prepared to talk, when appropriate, and to fight, if necessary. Every member of NATO stands with us in a common commitment to preserve this symbol of free man's will to remain free.

I cannot now predict the course of future negotiations over Berlin. I can only say that we are sparing no honorable effort to find a peaceful and mutually acceptable resolution of this problem. I believe such a resolution can be found, and with it an improvement in our relations with the Soviet Union, if only the leaders in the Kremlin will recognize the basic rights and interests involved, and the interest of all mankind in peace.

But the Atlantic Community is no longer concerned with purely military aims. As its common undertakings grow at an ever-increasing pace, we are, and increasingly will be, partners in aid, trade, defense, diplomacy, and monetary affairs.

The emergence of the new Europe is being matched by the emergence of new ties across the Atlantic. It is a matter of undramatic daily cooperation in hundreds of workaday tasks: of currencies kept in effective relation, of development loans meshed together, of standardized weapons, and concerted diplomatic positions. The Atlantic Community grows, not like a volcanic mountain, by one mighty explosion, but like a coral reef, from the accumulating activity of all.

Thus, we in the free world are moving steadily toward unity and cooperation, in the teeth of that old Bolshevik prophecy, and at the very time when extraordinary rumbles of discord can be heard across the Iron Curtain. It is not free societies which bear within them the seeds of inevitable disunity.

On one special problem, of great concern to our friends, and to us, I am proud to give the Congress an encouraging report. Our efforts to safeguard the dollar are progressing. In the 11 months preceding last February 1, we suffered a new loss of nearly $2 billion in gold. In the 11 months that followed, the loss was just over half a billion dollars. And our deficit in our basic transactions with the rest of the world - trade, defense, foreign aid, and capital, excluding volatile short-term flows - has been reduced from $2 billion for 1960 to about one-third that amount for 1961. Speculative fever against the dollar is ending - and confidence in the dollar has been restored.

We did not - and could not - achieve these gains through import restrictions, troop withdrawals, exchange controls, dollar devaluation or choking off domestic recovery. We acted not in panic but in perspective. But the problem is not yet solved. Persistently large deficits would endanger our economic growth and our military and defense commitments abroad. Our goal must be a reasonable equilibrium in our balance of payments. With the cooperation of the Congress, business, labor, and our major allies, that goal can be reached.

We shall continue to attract foreign tourists and investments to our shores, to seek increased military purchases here by our allies, to maximize foreign aid procurement from American firms, to urge increased aid from other fortunate nations to the less fortunate, to seek tax laws which do not favor investment in other industrialized nations or tax havens, and to urge coordination of allied fiscal and monetary policies so as to discourage large and disturbing capital movements.

Above all, if we are to pay for our commitments abroad, we must expand our exports. Our businessmen must be export-conscious and export-competitive. Our tax policies must spur modernization of our plants - our wage and price gains must be consistent with productivity to hold the line on prices - our export credit and promotion campaigns for American industries must continue to expand.

But the greatest challenge of all is posed by the growth of the European Common Market. Assuming the accession of the United Kingdom, there will arise across the Atlantic a trading partner behind a single external tariff similar to ours with an economy which nearly equals our own. Will we in this country adapt our thinking to these new prospects and patterns - or will we wait until events have passed us by?

This is the year to decide. The Reciprocal Trade Act is expiring. We need a new law - a wholly new approach - a bold new instrument of American trade policy. Our decision could well affect the unity of the West, the course of the Cold War, and the economic growth of our Nation for a generation to come.

If we move decisively, our factories and farms can increase their sales to their richest, fastest-growing market. Our exports will increase. Our balance of payments position will improve. And we will have forged across the Atlantic a trading partnership with vast resources for freedom.

If, on the other hand, we hang back in deference to local economic pressures, we will find ourselves cut off from our major allies. Industries - and I believe this is most vital - industries will move their plants and jobs and capital inside the walls of the Common Market, and jobs, therefore, will be lost here in the United States if they cannot otherwise compete for its consumers. Our farm surpluses - our balance of trade, as you all know, to Europe, the Common Market, in farm products, is nearly three or four to one in our favor, amounting to one of the best earners of dollars in our balance of payments structure, and without entrance to this Market, without the ability to enter it, our farm surpluses will pile up in the Middle West, tobacco in the South, and other commodities, which have gone through Western Europe for 15 years. Our balance of payments position will worsen. Our consumers will lack a wider choice of goods at lower prices. And millions of American workers -

whose jobs depend on the sale or the transportation or the distribution of exports or imports, or whose jobs will be endangered by the movement of our capital to Europe, or whose jobs can be maintained only in an expanding economy - these millions of workers in your home States and mine will see their real interests sacrificed.

Members of the Congress: The United States did not rise to greatness by waiting for others to lead. This Nation is the world's foremost manufacturer, farmer, banker, consumer, and exporter. The Common market is moving ahead at an economic growth rate twice ours. The Communist economic offensive is under way. The opportunity is ours - the initiative is up to us and I believe that 1962 is the time.

To seize that initiative, I shall shortly send to the Congress a new five-year Trade Expansion Action, far-reaching in scope but designed with great care to make certain that its benefits to our people far outweigh any risks. The bill will permit the gradual elimination of tariffs here in the United States and in the Common Market on those items in which we together supply 80 percent of the world's trade - mostly items in which our own ability to compete is demonstrated by the fact that we sell abroad, in these items, substantially more than we import. This step will make it possible for our major industries to compete with their counterparts in Western Europe for access to European consumers.

On other goods the bill will permit a gradual reduction of duties up to 50 percent - permitting bargaining by major categories - and provide for appropriate and tested forms of assistance to firms and employees adjusting to import competition. We are not neglecting the safeguards provided by peril points, an escape clause, or the National Security Amendment. Nor are we abandoning our non-European friends or our traditional "most favored nation" principle. On the contrary, the bill will provide new encouragement for their sale of tropical agricultural products, so important to our friends in Latin America, who have long depended upon the European market, who now find themselves faced with new challenges which we must join with them in overcoming.

Concessions, in this bargaining, must of course be reciprocal, not unilateral. The Common Market will not fulfill its own high promise unless its outside tariff walls are low. The dangers of restriction or timidity in our own policy have counterparts for our friends in Europe. For together we face a common challenge: to enlarge the prosperity of free men everywhere - to build in partnership a new trading community in which all free nations may gain from the productive energy of free competitive effort.

These various elements in our foreign policy lead, as I have said, to a single goal - the goal of a peaceful world of free and independent states. This is our guide for the present and our vision for the future - a free community of nations, independent but interdependent, uniting north and south, east and west, in one great family of man, outgrowing and transcending the hates and fears that rend our age.

We will not reach that goal today, or tomorrow. We may not reach it in our own lifetime. But the quest is the greatest adventure of our century. We sometimes chafe at the burden of our obligations, the complexity of our decisions, the agony of our choices. But there is no comfort or security for us in evasion, no solution in abdication, no relief in irresponsibility.

A year ago, in assuming the tasks of the Presidency, I said that few generations, in all history, had been granted the role of being the great defender of freedom in its hour of maximum danger. This is our good fortune; and I welcome it now as I did a year ago. For it is the fate of this generation - of you in the Congress and of me as President - to live with a struggle we did not start, in a world we did not make. But the pressures of life are not always distributed by choice. And while no nation has ever faced such a challenge, no nation has ever been so ready to seize the burden and the glory of freedom.

And in this high endeavor, may God watch over the United States of America.

Nuclear Testing and Disarmament
Radio and Television Address
Washington, DC
March 2, 1962

Seventeen years ago man unleashed the power of the atom. He thereby took into his mortal hands the power of self-extinction. Throughout the years that have followed, under three successive Presidents, the United States has sought to banish this weapon from the arsenals of individual nations. For of all the awesome responsibilities entrusted to this office, none is more somber to contemplate than the special statutory authority to employ nuclear arms in the defense of our people and freedom.

But until mankind has banished both war and its instruments of destruction, the United States must maintain an cffcctive quantity and quality of nuclear weapons, so deployed and protected as to be capable of surviving any surprise attack and devastating the attacker. Only through such strength can we be certain of deterring a nuclear strike, or an overwhelming ground attack, upon our forces and our allies. Only through such strength can we in the free world - should that deterrent fail - face the tragedy of another war with any hope of survival. And that deterrent strength, if it is to be effective and credible when compared with that of any other nation, must embody the most modern, the most reliable and the most versatile nuclear weapons our research and development can produce.

The testing of new weapons and their effects is necessarily a part of that research and development process. Without tests - to experiment and verify -

progress is limited. A nation which is refraining from tests obviously cannot match the gains of a nation conducting tests. And when all nuclear powers refrain from testing, the nuclear arms race is held in check.

That is why this Nation has long urged an effective worldwide end to nuclear tests. And this is why in 1958 we voluntarily subscribed, as did the Soviet Union, to a nuclear test moratorium, during which neither side would conduct new nuclear tests, and both East and West would seek concrete plans for their control.

But on September first of last year, while the United States and the United Kingdom were negotiating in good faith at Geneva, the Soviet Union callously broke its moratorium with a two month series of tests of more than 40 nuclear weapons. Preparations for these tests had been secretly underway for many months. Accompanied by new threats and new tactics of terror, these tests - conducted mostly in the atmosphere - represented a major Soviet effort to put nuclear weapons back into the arms race.

Once it was apparent that new appeals and proposals were to no avail, I authorized on September fifth a resumption of U.S. nuclear tests underground, and I announced on November second - before the close of the Soviet series - that preparations were being ordered for a resumption of atmospheric tests, and that we would make whatever tests our security required in the light of Soviet gains.

This week, the National Security Council of the United States has completed its review of this subject. The scope of the Soviet tests has been carefully reviewed by the most competent scientists in the country. The scope and justification of proposed American tests have been carefully reviewed, determining which experiments can be safely deferred, which can be deleted, which can be combined or conducted underground, and which are essential to our military and scientific progress. Careful attention has been given to the limiting of radioactive fallout, to the future course of arms control diplomacy, and to our obligations to other nations.

Every alternative was examined. Every avenue of obtaining Soviet agreement was explored. We were determined not to rush into imitating their tests. And we were equally determined to do only what our own security required us to do. Although the complex preparations have continued at full speed while these facts were being uncovered, no single decision of this Administration has been more thoroughly or more thoughtfully weighed.

Having carefully considered these findings - having received the unanimous recommendations of the pertinent department and agency heads - and having observed the Soviet Union's refusal to accept any agreement which would inhibit its freedom to test extensively after preparing secretly - I have today authorized the Atomic Energy Commission and the Department of Defense to conduct a series of nuclear tests - beginning when our preparations are completed, in the latter part of April, and to be concluded as quickly as possible (within two or three months) - such series, involving only those tests which cannot be held underground, to take place in the atmosphere over the Pacific Ocean.

These tests are to be conducted under conditions which restrict the radioactive fallout to an absolute minimum, far less than the contamination created by last fall's Soviet series. By paying careful attention to location, wind and weather conditions, and by holding these tests over the open seas, we intend to rule out any problem of fallout in the immediate area of testing. Moreover, we will hold the increase in radiation in the Northern Hemisphere, where nearly all such fallout will occur, to a very low level.

Natural radioactivity, as everyone knows, has always been a part of the air around us, with certain long-range biological effects. By conservative estimate, the total effects from this test series will be roughly equal to only 1 percent of those due to this natural background. It has been estimated, in fact, that the exposure due to radioactivity from these tests will be less than 1/50 of the difference which can be experienced, due to variations in natural radioactivity, simply by living in different locations in our own country. This will obviously be well within the guides for general population health and safety, as set by the Federal Radiation Council; and considerably less than 1/10 of 1 percent of the exposure guides set for adults who work with industrial radioactivity.

Nevertheless, I find it deeply regrettable that any radioactive material must be added to the atmosphere - that even one additional individual's health may be risked in the foreseeable future. And however remote and infinitesimal those hazards may be, I still exceedingly regret the necessity of balancing these hazards against the hazards to hundreds of millions of lives which would be created by any relative decline in our nuclear strength.

In the absence of any major shift in Soviet policies, no American President - responsible for the freedom and the safety of so many people - could in good faith make any other decision. But because our nuclear posture affects the security of all Americans and all free men - because this issue has aroused such widespread concern - I want to share with you and all the world, to the fullest extent our security permits, all of the facts and the thoughts which have gone into this decision.

Many of these facts are hard to explain in simple terms - many are hard to face in a peaceful world - but these are facts which must be faced and must be understood.

Had the Soviet tests of last fall merely reflected a new effort in intimidation and bluff, our security would not have been affected. But in fact they also reflected a highly sophisticated technology, the trial of novel designs and techniques, and some substantial gains in weaponry. Many of these tests were aimed at improving their defenses against missiles - others were proof tests, trying out existing weapons systems - but over one-half emphasized the development of new weapons, particularly those of greater explosive power.

A primary purpose of these tests was the development of warheads which weigh very little compared to the destructive efficiency of their thermonuclear yield. One Soviet test weapon exploded with the force of 58 megatons - the equivalent of 58 million tons of TNT. This was a reduced-yield version of their much-publicized hundred-megaton bomb. Today, Soviet missiles do not appear able to carry so heavy a warhead. But there is no avoiding the fact that other Soviet tests, in the 1 to 5 megaton range and up, were aimed at unleashing increased destructive power in warheads actually capable of delivery by existing missiles.

Much has also been said about Soviet claims for an anti-missile missile. Some of the Soviet tests which measured the effects of high altitude nuclear explosion - in one case over 100 miles high - were related to this problem. While apparently seeking information on the effects of nuclear blasts on radar and communication, which is important in developing an anti-missile defense system, these tests did not, in our judgment, reflect a developed system.

In short, last fall's tests, in and by themselves, did not give the Soviet Union superiority in nuclear power. They did, however, provide the Soviet laboratories with a mass of data and experience on which, over the next two or three years, they can base significant analyses, experiments and extrapolations, preparing for the next test series which would confirm and advance their findings.

And I must report to you in all candor that further Soviet tests, in the absence of further Western progress, could well provide the Soviet Union with a nuclear attack and defense capability so powerful as to encourage aggressive designs. Were we to stand still while the Soviets surpassed us - or even appeared to surpass us - the Free World's ability to deter, to survive and to respond to an all-out attack would be seriously weakened.

The fact of the matter is that we cannot make similar strides without testing in the atmosphere as well as underground. For, in many areas of nuclear weapons research, we have reached the point where our progress is stifled without experiments in every environment. The information from our last series of atmospheric tests in

1958 has all been analyzed and re-analyzed. It cannot tell us more without new data. And it is in these very areas of research - missile penetration and missile defense - that further major Soviet tests, in the absence of further Western tests, might endanger our deterrent.

In addition to proof tests of existing systems, two different types of tests have therefore been decided upon. The *first* and most important are called "effect tests" - determining what effect an enemy nuclear explosion would have upon our ability to survive and respond. We are spending great sums of money on radar to alert our defenses and to develop possible anti-missile systems - on the communications which enable our command and control centers to direct a response - on hardening our missile sites, shielding our missiles and warheads from defensive action, and providing them with electronic guidance systems to find their targets. But we cannot be certain how much of this preparation will turn out to be useless: blacked out, paralyzed or destroyed by the complex effects of a nuclear explosion.

We know enough from earlier tests to be concerned about such phenomena. We know that the Soviets conducted such tests last fall. But until we measure the effects of actual explosions in the atmosphere under realistic conditions, we will not know precisely how to prepare our future defenses, how best to equip our missiles for penetration of an anti-missile system, or whether it is possible to achieve such a system for ourselves.

Second, we must test in the atmosphere to permit the development of those more advanced concepts and more effective, efficient weapons which, in the light of Soviet tests, are deemed essential to our security. Nuclear weapons technology is a constantly changing field. If our weapons are to be more secure, more flexible in their use and more selective in their impact - if we are to be alert to new breakthroughs, to experiment with new designs - if we are to maintain our scientific momentum and leadership - then our weapons progress must not be limited to theory or to the confines of laboratories and caves.

This series is designed to lead to many important, if not always dramatic, results. Improving the nuclear yield per pound of weight in our weapons will make them easier to move, protect and fire - more likely to survive a surprise attack - and more adequate for effective retaliation. It will also, even more importantly, enable us to add to our missiles certain penetration aids and decoys, and to make those missiles effective at high altitude detonations, in order to render ineffective any anti-missile or interceptor system an enemy might some day develop.

Whenever possible, these development tests will be held underground. But the larger explosions can only be tested in the atmosphere. And while our technology in smaller weapons is unmatched, we now know that the Soviets have made major gains in developing larger weapons of low weight and high explosive content - of 1 to 5 megatons and upward. Fourteen of their tests last fall were in this category, for a total of 30 such tests over the years. The United States, on the other hand, had conducted, prior to the moratorium, a total of only 20 tests within this megaton range.

While we will be conducting far fewer tests than the Soviets, with far less fallout, there will still be those in other countries who will urge us to refrain from testing at all. Perhaps they forget that this country long refrained from testing, and sought to ban all tests, while the Soviets were secretly preparing new explosions. Perhaps they forget the Soviet threats of last autumn and their arbitrary rejection of all appeals and proposals, from both the United States and the United Nations. But those free peoples who value their freedom and their security, and look to our relative strength to shield them from danger - those who know of our good faith in seeking an end to testing and an end to the arms race - will, I am confident, want the United States to do whatever it must do to deter the threat of aggression.

If they felt we could be swayed by threats of intimidation - if they thought we could permit a repetition of last summer's deception - then surely they would lose faith in our will and our wisdom as well as our weaponry. I have no doubt that most of our friends around the world have shared my own hope that we would never find it necessary to test again - and my own belief that, in the long run, the only real security in this age of nuclear peril rests not in armament but in disarmament. But I am equally certain that they would insist on our testing once that is deemed necessary to protect free world security. They know we are not deciding to test for political or psychological reasons - and they also know that we cannot avoid such tests for political or psychological reasons.

The leaders of the Soviet Union are also watching this decision. Should we fail to follow the dictates of our own security, they will chalk it up, not to goodwill, but to a failure of will - not to our confidence in Western superiority, but to our fear of world opinion, the very world opinion for which they showed such contempt. They could well be encouraged by such signs of weakness to seek another period of no testing without controls - another opportunity for stifling our progress while secretly preparing, on the basis of last fall's experiments, for the new test series which might alter the balance of power. With such a one-sided advantage, why would they change their strategy, or refrain from testing, merely because we refrained? Why would they want to halt their drive to surpass us in nuclear technology? And why would they ever consider accepting a true test ban or mutual disarmament?

Our reasons for testing and our peaceful intentions are clear - so clear that even the Soviets could not objectively regard our resumption of tests, following their own resumption of tests, as provocative or preparatory for war. On the contrary, it is my hope that the prospects for peace may actually be strengthened by this decision - once the Soviet leaders realize that the West will no longer stand still, negotiating in good faith, while they reject inspection and are free to prepare for further tests. As new disarmament talks approach, the basic lesson of some three years and 353 negotiating sessions at Geneva is this - that the Soviets will not agree to an effective ban on nuclear tests as long as a new series of offers and prolonged negotiations, or a new uninspected moratorium, or a new agreement without controls, would enable them once again to prevent the West from testing while they prepare in secret.

But inasmuch as this choice is now no longer open to them, let us hope that they will take a different attitude on banning nuclear tests - that they will prefer to see the nuclear arms race checked instead of intensified, with all the dangers that that intensification brings: the spread of nuclear weapons to other nations; the constant increase in world tensions; the steady decrease in all prospects for disarmament; and, with it, a steady decrease in the security of us all.

If the Soviets should change their position, we will have an opportunity to learn it immediately. On the 14th of March, in Geneva, Switzerland, a new 18-power conference on disarmament will begin. A statement of agreed principles has been worked out with the Soviets and endorsed by the U.N. In the long run, it is the constructive possibilities of this conference - and not the testing of new destructive weapons - on which rest the hopes of all mankind. However dim those hopes may sometimes seem, they can never be abandoned. And however far-off most steps toward disarmament appear, there are some that can be taken at once.

The United States will offer at the Geneva conference - not in the advance expectation they will be rejected, and not merely for purposes of propaganda - a series of concrete plans for a major "breakthrough to peace." We hope and believe that they will appeal to all nations opposed to war. They will include specific proposals for fair and enforceable agreements: to halt the production of fissionable materials and nuclear weapons and their transfer to other nations - to convert them from weapon stockpiles to peaceable uses - to destroy the warheads and the delivery systems that threaten man's existence - to check the dangers of surprise and accidental attack - to reserve outer space for peaceful use - and progressively to reduce all armed forces in such a way as ultimately to remove forever all threats and thoughts of war.

And of greatest importance to our discussion tonight, we shall, in association with the United Kingdom, present once again our proposals for a separate comprehensive treaty - with appropriate arrangements for detection and verification - to halt permanently the testing of all nuclear weapons, in every environment: in the air, in outer space, under ground and under water. New modifications will also be offered in the light of new experience.

The essential arguments and facts relating to such a treaty are well-known to the Soviet Union. There is no need for further repetition, propaganda or delay. The fact that both sides have decided to resume testing only emphasizes the need for new agreement, not new argument. And before charging that this decision shatters all hopes for agreement, the Soviets should recall that we were willing to work out with them, for joint submission to the United Nations, an agreed statement of disarmament principles at the very time their autumn tests were being conducted. And Mr. Khrushchev knows, as he said in 1960, that any nation which broke the moratorium could expect other nations to be "forced to take the same road."

Our negotiators will be ready to talk about this treaty even before the Conference begins on March 14th - and they will be ready to sign well before the date on which our tests are ready to begin. That date is still nearly two months away. If the Soviet Union should now be willing to accept such a treaty, to sign it before the latter part of April, and apply it immediately - if all testing can thus be actually halted - then the nuclear arms race would be slowed down at last - the security of the United States and its ability to meet its commitments would be safeguarded - and there would be no need for our tests to begin.

But this must be a fully effective treaty. We know now enough about broken negotiations, secret preparations, and the advantages gained from a long test series never to offer again an uninspected moratorium. Some may urge us to try it again, keeping our preparations to test in a constant state of readiness. But in actual practice, particularly in a society of free choice, we cannot keep top-flight scientists concentrating on the preparation of an experiment which may or may not take place on an uncertain date in the undefined future. Nor can large technical laboratories be kept fully alert on a stand-by basis waiting for some other nation to break an agreement. This is not merely difficult or inconvenient - we have explored this alternative thoroughly, and found it impossible of execution.

In short, in the absence of a firm agreement that would halt nuclear tests by the latter part of April, we shall go ahead with our talks - striving for some new avenue of agreement - but we shall also go ahead with our tests. If, on the other hand, the Soviet Union should accept such a treaty in the opening month of talks, that single step would be a monumental step toward peace - and both Prime Minister Macmillan and I would think it fitting to meet Chairman Khruschchev at Geneva to sign the final pact.

For our ultimate objective is not to test for the sake of testing. Our real objective is to make our own tests unnecessary, to prevent others from testing, to prevent the nuclear arms race from mushrooming out of control, to take the first steps toward general and complete disarmament. And that is why, in the last analysis, it is the leaders of the Soviet Union who must bear the heavy responsibility of choosing, in the weeks that lie ahead, whether we proceed with these steps - or proceed with new tests.

If they are convinced that their interests can no longer be served by the present course of events, then it is my fervent hope that they will agree to an effective treaty. But if they persist in rejecting all means of true inspection, then we shall be left with no choice but to keep our own defensives arsenal adequate for the security of all free men.

It is our hope and prayer that these grim, unwelcome tests will never have to be made - that these deadly weapons will never have to be fired - and that our preparations for war will bring about the preservation of peace. Our foremost aim is the control of force, not the pursuit of force, in a world made safe for mankind. But whatever the future brings, I am sworn to uphold and defend the freedom of the American people - and I intend to do whatever must be done to fulfill that solemn obligation.

Address at
The University of California
Berkeley, California
March 23, 1962

The last time that I came to this Stadium was 22 years ago, when I visited it in November of 1940 as a student at a nearby small school for the game with Stanford. And we got a - I must say I had a much warmer reception today than I did from my Coast friends here on that occasion. In those days we used to fill these universities for football, and now we do it for academic events, and I'm not sure that this doesn't represent a rather dangerous trend for the future of our country.

I am delighted to be here on this occasion for though it is the 94th anniversary of the Charter, in a sense this is the hundredth anniversary. For this university and so many other universities across our country owe their birth to the most extraordinary piece of legislation which this country has ever adopted, and that is the Morrill Act, signed by President Abraham Lincoln in the darkest and most uncertain days of the Civil War, which set before the country the opportunity to build the great land-grant colleges, of which this is so distinguished a part. Six years later, this university obtained its Charter.

In its first graduating class it included a future Governor of California, a future Congressman, a judge, a State assemblyman, a clergyman, a lawyer, a doctor - all in a graduating class of 12 students!

This college, therefore, from its earliest beginnings, has recognized, and its graduates have recognized, that the purpose of education is not merely to advance the economic self-interest of its graduates. The people of California, as much if not more than the people of any other State, have supported their colleges and their universities and their schools, because they recognize how important it is to the maintenance of a free society that its citizens be well educated.

"Every man," said Professor Woodrow Wilson, "sent out from a university should be a man of his nation as well as a man of his time."

And Prince Bismarck was even more specific. One third, he said, of the students of German universities broke down from overwork, another third broke down from dissipation, and the other third ruled Germany.

I do not know which third of students are here today, but I am confident that I am talking to the future leaders of this State and country who recognize their responsibilities to the public interest.

Today we carry on that tradition. Our distinguished and courageous Secretary of Defense, our distinguished Secretary of State, the Chairman of the Atomic Energy Commission, the Director of the CIA and others, all are graduates of this University. It is a disturbing fact to me, and it may be to some of you, that the New Frontier owes as much to Berkeley as it does to Harvard University.

This has been a week of momentous events around the world. The long and painful struggle in Algeria which comes to an end. Both nuclear powers and neutrals labored at Geneva for a solution to the problem of a spiraling arms race, and also to the problems that so vex our relations with the Soviet Union. The Congress opened hearings on a trade bill, which is far more than a trade bill, but an opportunity to build a stronger and closer Atlantic Community. And my wife had her first and last ride on an elephant!

But history may well remember this as a week for an act of lesser immediate impact, and that is the decision by the United States and the Soviet Union to seek concrete agreements on the joint exploration of space. Experience has taught us that an agreement to negotiate does not always mean a negotiated agreement. But should such a joint effort be realized, its significance could well be tremendous for us all. In terms of space science, our combined knowledge and efforts can benefit the people of all the nations: joint weather satellites to provide more ample warnings against destructive storms - joint communications systems to draw the world more closely together and cooperation in space medicine research and space tracking operations to speed the day when man will go to the moon and beyond.

But the scientific gains from such a joint effort would offer, I believe, less realized return than the gains for world peace. For a cooperative Soviet-American effort in space science and exploration would emphasize the interests that must unite us, rather than those that always divide us. It offers us an area in which the stale and sterile dogmas of the cold war could be literally left a quarter of a million miles behind. And it would remind us on both sides that knowledge, not hate, is the passkey to the future - that knowledge transcends national antagonisms - that it speaks a universal language - that it is the possession, not of a single class, or of a single nation or a single ideology, but of all mankind.

I need hardly emphasize the happy pursuit of knowledge in this place. Your faculty includes more Nobel laureates than any other faculty in the world - more in this one community than our principal adversary has received since the awards began in 1901. And we take pride in that, only from a national point of view, because it indicates, as the Chancellor pointed out, the great intellectual benefits of a free society. This University of California will continue to grow as an intellectual center because your presidents and your chancellors and your professors have rigorously defended that unhampered freedom of discussion and inquiry which is the soul of the intellectual enterprise and the heart of a free university.

We may be proud as a nation of our record in scientific achievement - but at the same time we must be impressed by the interdependence of all knowledge. I am certain that every scholar and scientist here today would agree that his own work has benefitted immeasurably from the work of the men and women in other countries. The prospect of a partnership with Soviet scientists in the exploration of space opens up exciting prospects of collaboration in other areas of learning. And cooperation in the pursuit of knowledge can hopefully lead to cooperation in the pursuit of peace.

Yet the pursuit of knowledge itself implies a world where men are free to follow out the logic of their own ideas. It implies a world where nations are free to solve their own problems and to realize their own ideals. It implies, in short, a world where collaboration emerges from the voluntary decisions of nations strong in their own independence and their own self-respect. It implies, I believe, the kind of world which is emerging before our eyes - the world produced by the revolution of national independence which has today, and has been since 1945, sweeping across the face of the world.

I sometimes think that we are too much impressed by the clamor of daily events. The newspaper headlines and the television screens give us a short view. They so flood us with the stop-press details of daily stories that we lose sight of one of the great movements of history. Yet it is the profound tendencies of history and not the passing excitements, that will shape our future.

The short view gives us the impression as a nation of being shoved and harried, everywhere on the defense. But this impression is surely an optical illusion. From the perspective of Moscow, the world today may seem ever more troublesome, more intractable, more frustrating than it does to us. The leaders of the Communist world are confronted not only by acute internal problems in each Communist country - the failure of agriculture, the rising discontent of the youth and the intellectuals, the demands of technical and managerial groups for status and security. They are confronted in addition by profound divisions within the Communist world itself divisions which have already shattered the image of Communism as a universal system guaranteed to abolish all social and international conflicts - the most valuable asset the Communists had for many years.

Wisdom requires the long view. And the long view shows us that the revolution of national independence is a fundamental fact of our era. This revolution will not be stopped. As new nations emerge from the oblivion of centuries, their first aspiration is to affirm their national identity. Their deepest hope is for a world where, within a framework of international cooperation, every country can solve its own problems according to its own traditions and ideals.

It is in the interests of the pursuit of knowledge - and it is in our own national interest - that this revolution of national independence succeed. For the Communists rest everything on the idea of a monolithic world - a world where all knowledge has a single pattern, all societies move toward a single model, and all problems and roads have a single solution and a single destination. The pursuit of knowledge, on the other hand, rests everything on the opposite idea - on the idea of a world based on diversity, self-determination, freedom. And that is the kind of world to which we Americans, as a nation, are committed by the principles upon which the great Republic was founded.

As men conduct the pursuit of knowledge, they create a world which freely unites national diversity and international partnership. This emerging world is incompatible with the Communist world order. It will irresistibly burst the bonds of the Communist organization and the Communist ideology. And diversity and independence, far from being opposed to the American conception of world order, represent the very essence of our view of the future of the world.

There used to be so much talk a few years ago about the inevitable triumph of communism. We hear such talk much less now. No one who examines the modern world can doubt that the great currents of history are carrying the world away from the monolithic idea towards the pluralistic idea - away from communism and towards national independence and freedom. No one can doubt that the wave of the future is not the conquest of the world by a single dogmatic creed but the liberation of the diverse energies of free nations and free men. No one can doubt that cooperation in the pursuit of knowledge must lead to freedom of the mind and freedom of the soul.

Beyond the drumfire of daily crisis, therefore, there is arising the outlines of a robust and vital world community, founded on nations secure in their own independence, and united by allegiance to world peace. It would be foolish to say that this world will be won tomorrow, or the day after. The processes of history are fitful and uncertain and aggravating. There will be frustrations and setbacks. There will be times of anxiety and gloom. The specter of thermonuclear war will continue to hang over mankind; and we must heed the advice of Oliver Wendell Holmes of "freedom leaning on her spear" until all nations are wise enough to disarm safely and effectively.

Yet we can have a new confidence today in the direction in which history is moving. Nothing is more stirring than the recognition of great public purpose. Every great age is marked by innovation and daring - by the ability to meet unprecedented problems with intelligent solutions. In a time of turbulence and change, it is more true than ever that knowledge is power; for only by true understanding and steadfast judgment are we able to master the challenge of history.

If this is so, we must strive to acquire knowledge - and to apply it with wisdom. We must reject oversimplified theories of international life - the theory that American power is unlimited, or that the American mission is to remake the world in the American image. We must seize the vision of a free and diverse world - and shape our policies to speed progress toward a more flexible world order.

This is the unifying spirit of our policies in the world today. The purpose of our aid programs must be to help developing countries move forward as rapidly as possible on the road to genuine national independence. Our military policies must assist nations to protect the processes of democratic reform and development against disruption and intervention. Our diplomatic policies must strengthen our relations with the whole world, with our several alliances and within the United Nations.

As we press forward on every front to realize a flexible world order, the role of the university becomes ever more important, both as a reservoir of ideas and as a repository of the long view of the shore dimly seen.

"Knowledge is the great sun of the firmament," said Senator Daniel Webster. "Life and power are scattered with all its beams."

In its light, we must think and act not only for the moment but for our time. I am reminded of the story of the greaat French Marshal Lyautey, who once asked his gardener to plant a tree. The gardener objected that the tree was slow-growing and would not reach maturity for a hundred years. The Marshal replied, "In that case, there is no time to lose, plant it this afternoon."

Today a world of knowledge - a world of cooperation - a just and lasting peace - may be years away. But we have no time to lose. Let us plant our trees this afternoon.

Remarks at a Dinner Honoring Nobel Prize Winners of the Western Hemisphere Washington, DC April 29, 1962

I want to welcome you to the White House. Mr. Lester Pearson informed me that a Canadian newspaperman said yesterday that this is the President's "Easter egghead roll on the White House lawn." I want to deny that!

I want to tell you how welcome you are to the White House. I think this is the most extraordinary collection of talent, of human knowledge, that has ever been gathered together at the White House, with the possible exception of when Thomas Jefferson dined alone.

Someone once said that Thomas Jefferson was a gentleman of 32 who could calculate an eclipse, survey an estate, tie an artery, plan an edifice, try a cause, break a horse, and dance the minuet. Whatever he may have lacked, if he could have had his former colleague, Mr. Franklin, here we all would have been impressed.

In any case, I am delighted to welcome you here. We are delighted to have the Norwegian Ambassador and the Swedish Minister to represent their governments, and we are delighted to have the Nobel prize winners of the Western Hemisphere here at this dinner.

I know that the Nobel prize does not have any geographic or national implications. Mr. Nobel in his will, in fact, made it very clear when he said that he hoped that in the giving of the prize that no attention would be paid to nationality. He declared it to be "my express desire that in awarding the prize, no consideration whatsoever be paid to the nationality of the candidates; that is to say, the most deserving be awarded the prize, whether he or she be Scandinavian or not."

In any case, there is no nationality in the Nobel prize, just as there is no nationality in the acquisition of knowledge. I know that every man here who has won the Nobel prize, not only does he build on the past, which goes back hundreds and thousands of years, on the efforts of other men and women, but he also builds on the efforts of those in other countries; and therefore, quite rightly, the Nobel prize has no national significance.

But I think we can take some satisfaction that this hemisphere has been able to develop an atmosphere which has permitted the happy pursuit of knowledge, and of peace; and that over 40 percent of the Nobel prizes in the last 30 years have gone to men and women in this hemisphere.

And of particular pleasure today is the fact that 13 Nobel prizes for peace have gone to those who live in this hemisphere. I think the pursuit of knowledge, the pursuit of peace, are very basic drives and pressures in this life of ours - and this dinner is an attempt, in a sense, to recognize those great efforts, to encourage young Americans and young people in this hemisphere to develop the same drive and deep desire for knowledge and peace.

So I want you to know that you are most welcome here. I regard this as the most distinguished and significant dinner that we have had in the White House since I have been here, and I think in many, many years.

And I hope that it will stimulate among all people, in this hemisphere and far beyond, the recognition of the close ties that bind all who labor to provide a better life for their people.

So I hope that you will join me in drinking to the Nobel prize winners of this year and other years - and perhaps more widely, to all those people everywhere whom they serve.

Commencement Address
United States Military Academy
West Point, New York
June 6, 1962

I want to express my appreciation for your generous invitation to come to this graduating class. I am sure that all of you who sit here today realize, particularly in view of the song we have just heard, that you are part of a long tradition stretching back to the earliest days of this country's history, and that where you sit sat once some of the most celebrated names in our Nation's history, and also some who are not so well known, but who, on 100 different battlefields in many wars involving every generation of this country's history, have given very clear evidence of their commitment to their country.

So that I know you feel a sense of pride in being part of that tradition, and as a citizen of the United States, as well as President, I want to express our high regard to all of you in appreciation for what you are doing and what you will do for our country in the days ahead.

I would also like to announce at this time that as Commander in Chief I am exercising my privilege of directing the Secretary of the Army and the Superintendent of West Point to remit all existing confinements and other cadet punishments, and I hope that it will be possible to carry this out today.

General Westmoreland was slightly pained to hear that this was impending in view of the fact that one cadet, who I am confident will some day be the head of the Army, has just been remitted for 8 months, and is about to be released. But I am glad to have the opportunity to participate in the advancement of his military career.

My own confinement goes for another two and a half years, and I may ask for it to be extended instead of remitted.

I want to say that I wish all of you, the graduates, success. While I say that, I am not unmindful of the fact that two graduates of this Academy have reached the White House, and neither was a member of my party. Until I am more certain that this trend will be broken, I wish that all of you may be generals and not Commanders in Chief.

I want to say that I am sure you recognize that your schooling is only interrupted by today's occasion and not ended, because the demands that will be made upon you in the service of your country in the coming months and years will be really more pressing, and in many ways more burdensome, as well as more challenging, than ever before in our history. I know that many of you may feel, and many of our citizens may feel, that in these days of the nuclear age, when the war may last in its final form a day or two or three days before much of the world is burned up, that your service to your country will be only standing and waiting. Nothing, of course, could be further from the truth. I am sure that many Americans believe that the days before World War II were the golden age when the stars were falling on all the graduates of West Point, that that was the golden time of service, and that you have moved into a period where military service, while vital, is not as challenging as it was then. Nothing could be further from the truth.

The fact of the matter is that the period just ahead in the next decade will offer more opportunities for service to the graduates of this Academy than ever before in the history of the United States, because all around the world, in countries which are heavily engaged in the maintenance of their freedom, graduates of this Academy are heavily involved. Whether it is in Viet Nam or in Laos or in Thailand, whether it is a military advisory group in Iran, whether it is a military attache is some Latin American country during a difficult and challenging period, whether it is the commander of our troops in South Korea - the burdens that will be placed upon you when you fill those positions as you must inevitably, will require more from you than ever before in our history. The graduates of West Point, the Naval Academy, and the Air Academy in the next 10 years will have the greatest opportunity for the defense of freedom that this Academy's graduates have ever had. And I am sure that the Joint Chiefs of Staff endorse that view, knowing as they do and I do, the heavy burdens that are required of this Academy's graduates have every day - General Tucker in Laos, or General Harkins in Viet Nam, and a dozen others who hold key and significant positions involving the security of the United States and the defense of freedom. You are going to follow in their footsteps and I must say that I think that you will be privileged in the years ahead to find yourselves so heavily involved in the great interests of this country.

Therefore, I hope that you realize - and I hope every American realizes - how much we depend upon you. Your strictly military responsibilities, therefore, will require a versatility and an adaptability never before required in either war or in peace. They may involve the command and control of modern nuclear weapons and modern delivery systems, so complex that only a few scientists can understand their operation, so devastating that their inadvertent use would be of worldwide concern, but so new that their employment and their effects have never been tested in combat conditions.

On the other hand, your responsibilities may involve the command of more traditional forces, but in less traditional roles. Men risking their lives, not as combatants, but as instructors or advisers, or as symbols of our Nation's commitments. The fact that the United States is not directly at war in these areas in no way diminishes the skill and the courage that will be required, the service to our country which is rendered, or the pain of the casualties which are suffered.

To cite one final example of the range of responsibilities that will fall upon you: you may hold a position of command with our special forces, forces which are too unconventional to be called conventional, forces which are growing in number and importance and significance, for we now know that it is wholly misleading to call this "the nuclear age," or to say that our security rests only on the doctrine of massive retaliation.

Korea has not been the only battleground since the end of the Second World War. Men have fought and died in Malaya, in Greece, in the Philippines, in Algeria and Cuba and Cyprus, and almost continuously on the Indo-Chinese Peninsula. No nuclear weapons have been fired. No massive nuclear retaliation has been considered appropriate. This is another type of war, new in its intensity, ancient in its origin - war by guerrillas, subversives, insurgents, assassins, war by ambush instead of by combat; by infiltration, instead of aggression, seeking victory by eroding and exhausting the enemy instead of engaging him. It is a form of warfare uniquely adapted to what has been strangely called "wars of liberation," to undermine the efforts of new and poor countries to maintain the freedom that they have finally achieved. It preys on economic unrest and ethnic conflicts. It requires in those situations where we must counter it, and these are the kinds of challenges that will be before us in the next decade if freedom is to be saved, a whole new kind of strategy, a wholly different kind of force, and therefore a new and wholly different kind of military training.

But I have spoken thus far only of the military challenges which your education must prepare you for. The nonmilitary problems which you will face will also be most demanding, diplomatic, political, and economic. In the years ahead, some of you will serve as advisers to foreign aid missions or even to foreign governments. Some will negotiate terms of a ceasefire with broad political as well as military ramifications. Some of you will go to the far corners of the earth, and to the far reaches of space. Some of you will sit in the highest councils of the Pentagon. Others will hold delicate command posts which are international in character. Still others will advise on plans to abolish arms instead of using them to abolish others. Whatever your position, the scope of your decisions will not be confined to the traditional tenets of military competence and training. You will need to know and understand not only the foreign policy of the United States but the foreign policy of all countries scattered around the world who 20 years ago were the most distant names to us. You will need to give orders in different tongues and read maps by different systems. You will be involved in economic judgments which most economists would hesitate to make. At what point, for example, does military aid become burdensome to a country and make its freedom endangered rather than helping to secure it? To what extent can the gold and dollar cost of our overseas deployments be offset by foreign procurement? Or at what stage can a new weapons system be considered sufficiently advanced to justify large dollar appropriations?

In many countries, your posture and performance will provide the local population with the only evidence of what our country is really like. In other countries, your military mission, its advice and action, will play a key role in determining whether those people will remain free. You will need to understand the importance of military power and also the limits of military power, to decide what arms should be used to fight and when they should be used to prevent a fight, to determine what represents our vital interests and what interests are only marginal.

Above all, you will have a responsibility to deter war as well as to fight it. For the basic problems facing the world today are not susceptible of a final military solution. While we will long require the services and admire the dedication and commitment of the fighting men of this country, neither our strategy nor our psychology as a nation, and certainly not our economy, must become permanently dependent upon an ever-increasing military establishment.

Our forces, therefore, must fulfill a broader role as a complement to our diplomacy, as an arm of our diplomacy, as a deterrent to our adversaries, and as a symbol to our allies of our determination to support them.

That is why this Academy has seen its curriculum grow and expand in dimension, in substance, and in difficulty. That is why you cannot possibly have crowded into these 4 busy years all of the knowledge and all of the range of experience which you must bring to these subtle and delicate tasks which I have described. And that is why you will go to school year after year so you can serve this country to the best of your ability and your talent.

To talk of such talent and effort raises in the minds, I am sure, of everyone, and the minds of all of our countrymen, why - why should men such as you, able to master the complex arts of science, mathematics, language, economy, and all the rest devote their lives to a military career, with all of its risks and hardships? Why should their families be expected to make the personal and financial sacrifices that a military career inevitably brings with it? When there is a visible enemy to fight in open combat, the answer is not so difficult. Many serve, all applaud, and the tide of patriotism runs high. But when there is a long, slow struggle, with no immediate visible foe, your choice will seem hard indeed. And you will recall, I am sure, the lines found in an old sentry box in Gibraltar:

> God and the soldier all men adore
> In time of trouble and no more,
> For when war is over, and all things righted,
> God is neglected and the old soldier slighted.

But you have one satisfaction, however difficult those days may be: when you are asked by a President of the United States or by any other American what you are doing for your country, no man's answer will be clearer than your own. And that moral motivation which brought you here in the first place is part of your training here as well. West Point was not built to produce technical experts alone. It was built to produce men committed to the defense of their country, leaders of men who understand the great stakes which are involved, leaders who can be entrusted with the heavy responsibility which modern weapons and the fight for freedom entail, leaders who can inspire in their men the same sense of obligation to duty which you bring to it.

There is no single slogan that you can repeat to yourself in hard days or give to those who may be associated with you. In times past, a simple phrase, "54-40 or fight" or "to make the world safe for democracy" - that was enough. But the times, the weapons, and the issues are now more complicated than ever.

Eighteen years ago today, Ernie Pyle, describing those tens of thousands of young men who crossed the "ageless and indifferent" sea of the English Channel, searched in vain for a word to describe what they were fighting for. And finally he concluded that they were at least fighting for each other.

You and I leave here today to meet our separate responsibilities, to protect our Nation's vital interests by peaceful means if possible, by resolute action if necessary. And we go forth confident of support and success because we know that we are working and fighting for each other and for all those men and women all over the globe who are determined to be free.

Commencement Address
Yale University
New Haven, Connecticut
June 11, 1962

Let me begin by expressing my appreciation for the very deep honor that you have conferred upon me. As General de Gaulle occasionally acknowledges America to be the daughter of Europe, so I am pleased to come to Yale, the daughter of Harvard. It might be said now that I have the best of both worlds, a Harvard education and a Yale degree.

I am particularly glad to become a Yale man because as I think about my troubles, I find that a lot of them have come from other Yale men. Among businessmen, I have had a minor disagreement with Roger Blough, of the law school class of 1931, and I have had some complaints, too, from by friend Henry Ford, of the class of 1940. In journalism I seem to have a difference with John Hay Whitney, of the class of 1926 - and sometimes I also displease Henry Luce of the class of 1920, not to mention also William F. Buckley, Jr., of the class of 1950. I even have some trouble with my Yale advisers. I get along with them, but I am not always sure how they get along with each other.

I have the warmest feelings for Chester Bowles of the class of 1924, and for Dean Acheson of the class of 1915, and my assistant, McGeorge Bundy, of the class of 1940. But I am not 100 percent sure that these three wise and experienced Yale men wholly agree with each other on every issue.

So this administration which aims at peaceful cooperation among all Americans has been the victim of a certain natural pugnacity developed in this city among Yale men. Now that I, too, am a Yale man, it is time for peace. Last week at West Point, I availed myself of the powers of Commander in Chief to remit all sentences of offending cadets. In that same spirit, and in the historic tradition of Yale, let me now offer to smoke the clay pipe of friendship with all of my brother Elis, and I hope that they may be friends not only with me but even with each other.

In any event, I am very glad to be here and, as a new member of the club, I have been checking to see what earlier links existed between the institution of the Presidency and Yale. I found that a member of the class of 1878, William Howard Taft, served one term in the White House as preparation for becoming a member of this faculty. And a graduate of 1804, John C. Calhoun, regarded the Vice Presidency, quite naturally, as too lowly a status for a Yale alumnus - and became the only man in history to ever resign that office.

Calhoun in 1804 and Taft in 1878 graduated into a world very different from ours today. They and their contemporaries spent entire careers stretching over 40 years in grappling with a few dramatic issues on which the Nation was sharply and emotionally divided, issues that occupied the attention of a generation at a time: the national bank, the disposal of the public lands, nullification or union, freedom or slavery, gold or silver. Today these old sweeping issues very largely have disappeared. The central domestic issues of our time are more subtle and less simple. They relate not to basic clashes of philosophy or ideology but to ways and means of reaching common goals - to research for sophisticated solutions to complex and obstinate issues. The world of Calhoun, the world of Taft, had its own hard problems and notable challenges. But its problems are not our problems. Their age is not our age. As every past generation has had to disenthrall itself from an inheritance of truisms and stereotypes, so in our own time we must move on from the reassuring repetition of stale phrases to a new, difficult, but essential confrontation with reality.

For the great enemy of truth is very often not the lie - deliberate, contrived, and dishonest - but the myth - persistent, persuasive, and unrealistic. Too often we hold fast to the cliches of our forebears. We subject all facts to a prefabricated set of interpretations. We enjoy the comfort of opinion without the discomfort of thought.

Mythology distracts us everywhere - in government as in business, in politics as in economics, in foreign affairs as in domestic affairs. But today I want to particularly consider the myth and reality in our national economy. In recent months many have come to feel, as I do, that the dialog between the parties - between business and government, between the government and the public - is clogged by illusion and platitude and fails to reflect the true realities of contemporary American society.

I speak of these matters here at Yale because of the self-evident truth that a great university is always enlisted against the spread of illusion and on the side of reality. No one has said it more clearly than your President Griswold: "Liberal learning is both a safeguard against false ideas of freedom and a source of true ones." Your role as university men, whatever your calling, will be to increase each new generation's grasp of its duties.

There are three great areas of our domestic affairs in which, today, there is a danger that illusion may prevent effective action. They are, first, the question of the size and the shape of government's responsibilities; second, the question of public fiscal policy; and third, the matter of confidence, business confidence or public confidence, or simply confidence in America.

I want to talk about all three, and I want to talk about them carefully and dispassionately - and I emphasize that I am concerned here not with political debate but with finding ways to separate false problems from real ones.

If a contest in angry argument were forced upon it, no administration could shrink from response, and history does not suggest that American Presidents are totally without resources in an engagement forced upon them because of hostility in one sector of society. But in the wider national interest, we need not partisan wrangling but common concentration on common problems. I come here to this distinguished university to ask you to join in this great task.

Let us take first the question of the size and shape of government. The myth here is that government is big, and bad - and steadily getting bigger and worse. Obviously this myth has some excuse for existence. It is true that in recent history each new administration has spent much more money than its predecessor. Thus President Roosevelt outspent President Hoover, and with allowances for the special case of the Second World War, President Truman outspent President Roosevelt. Just to prove that this was not a partisan matter, President Eisenhower then outspent President Truman by the handsome figure of $182 billion. It is even possible, some think, that this trend may continue.

But does it follow from this that big government is growing relatively bigger? It does not - for the fact is for the last 15 years, the Federal Government - and also the Federal bureaucracy - have grown less rapidly than the economy as a whole. If we leave defense and space expenditures aside, the Federal Government since the Second World War has expanded less than any other major sector of our national life - less than industry, less than commerce, less than agriculture, less than higher education, and very much less than the noise about big government.

The truth about big government is the truth about any other great activity - it is complex. Certainly it is true that size brings dangers - but it is also true that size can bring benefits. Here at Yale, which has contributed so much to our national progress in science and medicine, it may be proper for me to mention one great and little noticed expansion of government which has brought strength to our whole society - the new role of our Federal Government as the major patron of research in science and in medicine. Few people realize that in 1961, in support of all university research in science and medicine, three dollars out of every four came from the Federal Government. I need hardly point out that this has taken place without undue enlargement of Government control - that American scientists remain second to none in their independence and in their individualism.

I am not suggesting that Federal expenditures cannot bring some measure of control. The whole thrust of Federal expenditures in agriculture have been related by purpose and design to control, as a means of dealing with the problems created by our farmers and our growing productivity. Each sector, my point is, of activity must be approached on its own merits and in terms of specific national needs. Generalities in regard to Federal expenditures, therefore, can be misleading - each case, science, urban renewal, education, agriculture, natural resources, each case must be determined on its merits if we are to profit from our unrivaled ability to combine the strength of public and private purpose.

Next, let us turn to the problem of our fiscal policy. Here the myths are legion and the truth hard to find. But let me take as a prime example the problem of the Federal budget. We persist in measuring our Federal fiscal integrity today by the conventional or administrative budget - with results which would be regarded as absurd in any business firm - in any country of Europe - or in any careful assessment of the reality of our national finances. The administrative budget has sound administrative uses. But for wider purposes it is less helpful. It omits our special trust funds and the effect that they have on our economy; it neglects changes in assets or inventories. It cannot tell a loan from a straight expenditure - and worst of all it cannot distinguish between operating expenditures and long-term investments.

This budget, in relation to the great problems of Federal fiscal policy which are basic to our economy in 1962, is not simply irrelevant; it can be actively misleading. And yet there is a mythology that measures all of our national soundness or unsoundness on the single simple basis of this same annual administrative budget. If our Federal budget is to serve not the debate but the country, we must and will find ways of clarifying this area of discourse.

Still in the area of fiscal policy, let me say a word about deficits. The myth persists that Federal deficits create inflation and budget surpluses prevent it. Yet sizeable budget surpluses after the war did not prevent inflation, and persistent deficits for the last several years have not upset our basic price stability. Obviously deficits are sometimes dangerous - and so are surpluses. But honest assessment plainly requires a more sophisticated view than the old and automatic cliche that deficits automatically bring inflation.

There are myths also about our public debt. It is widely supposed that this debt is growing at a dangerously rapid rate. In fact, both the debt per person and the debt as a proportion of our gross national product have declined sharply since the Second World War. In absolute terms the national debt since the end of World War II has increased only 8 percent, while private debt was increasing 305 percent, and the debts of State and local governments - on whom people frequently suggest we should place additional burdens - the debts of State and local governments have increased 378 percent. Moreover, debts, public and private, are neither good nor bad, in and of themselves. Borrowing can lead to overextension and collapse - but it can also lead to expansion and strength. There is no single, simple slogan in this field that we can trust.

Finally, I come to the problem of confidence. Confidence is a matter of myth and also a matter of truth - and this time let me take the truth of the matter first.

It is true - and of high importance - that the prosperity of this country depends on the assurance that all major elements within it will live up to their responsibilities. If business were to neglect its obligations to the public, if labor were blind to all public responsibility, above all, if government were to abandon its obvious - and statutory - duty of watchful concern for our economic health - if any of these things should happen, then confidence might well be weakened and the danger of stagnation would increase. This is the true issue of confidence.

But there is also the false issue - and its simplest form is the assertion that any and all unfavorable turns of the speculative wheel - however temporary and however plainly speculative in character - are the result of, and I quote, "a lack of confidence in the national administration." This I must tell you, while comforting, is not wholly true. Worse, it obscures the reality - which is also simple. The solid ground of mutual confidence is the necessary partnership of government with all of the sectors of our society in the steady quest for economic progress.

Corporate plans are not based on a political confidence in party leaders but on an economic confidence in the Nation's ability to invest and produce and consume. Business had full confidence in the administrations in power in 1929, 1954, 1958, and 1960 - but this was not enough to prevent recession when business lacked full confidence in the economy. What matters is the capacity of the Nation as a whole to deal with its economic problems and its opportunities.

The stereotypes I have been discussing distract our attention and divide our effort. These stereotypes do our Nation a disservice, not just because they are exhausted and irrelevant, but above all because they are misleading - because they stand in the way of the solution of hard and complicated facts. It is not new that past debates should obscure present realities. But the damage of such a false dialogue is greater today than ever before simply because today the safety of all the world - the very future of freedom - depends as never before upon the sensible and clearheaded management of the domestic affairs of the United States.

The real issues of our time are rarely as dramatic as the issues of Calhoun. The differences today are usually matters of degree. And we cannot understand and attack our contemporary problems in 1962 if we are bound by traditional labels and worn-out slogans of an earlier era. But the unfortunate fact of the matter is that our rhetoric has not kept pace with the speed of social and economic change. Our political debates, our public discourse - on current domestic and economic issues - too often bear little or no relation to the actual problems the United States faces.

What is at stake in our economic decisions today is not some grand warfare of rival ideologies which will sweep the country with passion but the practical management of a modern economy. What we need is not labels and cliches but more basic discussion of the sophisticated and technical questions involved in keeping a great economic machinery moving ahead.

The national interest lies in high employment and steady expansion of output, in stable prices, and a strong dollar. The declaration of such an objective is easy; their attainment in an intricate and interdependent economy and world is a little more difficult. To attain them, we require not some automatic response but hard thought. Let me end by suggesting a few of the real questions on our national agenda.

First, how can our budget and tax policies supply adequate revenues and preserve our balance of payments position without slowing up our economic growth?

Two, how are we to set our interest rates and regulate the flow of money in ways which will stimulate the economy at home, without weakening the dollar abroad? Given the spectrum of our domestic and international responsibilities, what should be the mix between fiscal and monetary policy?

Let me give several examples from my experience of the complexity of these matters and how political labels and ideological approaches are irrelevant to the solution.

Last week a distinguished graduate of this school, Senator Proxmire, of the class of 1938, who is ordinarily regarded as a liberal Democrat, suggested that we should follow in meeting our economic problems a stiff fiscal policy, with emphasis on budget balance and an easy monetary policy with low interest rates in order to keep our economy going. In the same week, the Bank of International Settlement in Basel, Switzerland, a conservative organization representing the central bankers of Europe suggested that the appropriate economic policy in the United States should be the very opposite; that we should follow a flexible budget policy, as in Europe, with deficits when the economy is down and a high monetary policy on interest rates, as in Europe, in order to control inflation and protect goals. Both may be right or wrong. It will depend on many different factors.

The point is that this is basically an administrative or executive problem in which political labels or cliches do not give us a solution.

A well-known business journal this morning, as I journeyed to New Haven, raised the prospects that a further budget deficit would bring inflation and encourage the flow of gold. We have had several budget deficits beginning with a $12-1/2 billion deficit in 1958, and it is true that in the fall of 1960 we had a gold dollar loss running at $5 billion annually. This would seem to prove the case that a deficit produces inflation and that we lose gold, yet there was no inflation following the deficit of 1958 nor has there been inflation since then.

Our wholesale price index since 1958 has remained completely level in spite of several deficits, because the loss of gold has been due to other reasons: price instability, relative interest rates, relative export-import balances, national security expenditures - all the rest.

Let me give you a third and final example. At the World Bank meeting in September, a number of American bankers attending predicted to their European colleagues that because of the fiscal 1962 budget deficit, there would be a strong inflationary pressure on the dollar and a loss of gold. Their predictions of inflation were shared by many in business and helped push the market up. The recent reality of non-inflation helped bring it down. We have had no inflation because we have had other factors in our economy that have contributed to price stability.

I do not suggest that the Government is right and they are wrong. The fact of the matter is in the Federal Reserve Board and in the administration this fall, a similar view was held by many well-informed and disinterested men that inflation was the major problem that we would face in the winter of 1962. But it was not. What I do suggest is that these problems are endlessly complicated and yet they go to the future of this country and its ability to prove to the world what we believe it must prove.

I am suggesting that the problems of fiscal and monetary policies in the sixties as opposed to the kinds of problems we faced in the thirties demand subtle challenges for which technical answers, not political answers, must be provided. These are matters upon which government and business may and in many cases will disagree. They are certainly matters that government and business should be discussing in the most sober, dispassionate, and careful way if we are to maintain the kind of vigorous economy upon which our country depends.

How can we develop and sustain strong and stable world markets for basic commodities without unfairness to the consumer and without undue stimulus to the producer? How can we generate the buying power which can consume what we produce on our farms and in our factories? How can we take advantage of the miracles of automation with the great demand that it will put upon highly skilled labor and yet offer employment to the half million of unskilled school dropouts each year who enter the labor market, eight million of them in the 1960's?

How do we eradicate the barriers which separate substantial minorities of our citizens from access to education and employment on equal terms with the rest?

How, in sum, can we make our free economy work at full capacity - that is, provide adequate profits for enterprise, adequate wages for labor, adequate utilization of plant, and opportunity for all?

These are the problems that we should be talking about - that the political parties and the various groups in our country should be discussing. They cannot be solved by incantations from the forgotten past. But the example of Western Europe shows that they are capable of solution - that governments, and many of them are conservative governments, prepared to face technical problems without ideological preconceptions, can coordinate the elements of a national economy and bring about growth and prosperity - a decade of it.

Some conversations I have heard in our own country sound like old records, long-playing, left over from the middle thirties. The debate of the thirties had its great significance and produced great results, but it took place in a different world with different needs and different tasks. It is our responsibility today to live in our own world, and to identify the needs and discharge the tasks of the 1960's.

If there is any current trend toward meeting present problems with old cliches, this is the moment to stop it - before it lands us all in a bog of sterile acrimony.

Discussion is essential; and I am hopeful that the debate of recent weeks, though up to now somewhat barren, may represent the start of a serious dialog of the kind which has led in Europe to such fruitful collaboration among all the elements of economic society and to a decade of unrivaled economic progress. But let us not engage in the wrong argument at the wrong time between the wrong people in the wrong country - while the real problems of our own time grow and multiply, fertilized by our neglect.

Nearly 150 years ago Thomas Jefferson wrote, "The new circumstances under which we are placed call for new words, new phrases, and for the transfer of old words to new objects." New words, new phrases, the transfer of old words to new objects - that is truer today than it was in the time of Jefferson, because the role of this country is so vastly more significant. There is a show in England called "Stop the World, I Want to Get Off." You have not chosen to exercise that option. You are part of the world and you must participate in these days of our years in the solution of the problems that pour upon us, requiring the most sophisticated and technical judgment; and as we work in consonance to meet the authentic problems of our times, we will generate a vision and an energy which will demonstrate anew to the world the superior vitality and the strength of the free society.

Address at Independence Hall
Philadelphia, Pennsylvania
July 4, 1962

It is a high honor for any citizen of our great Republic to speak at this Hall of Independence on this day of Independence. To speak as President of the United States to the Chief Executives of our 50 States is both an opportunity and an obligation. The necessity for comity between the National Government and the several States is an indelible lesson of our long history.

Because our system is designed to encourage both differences and dissent, because its checks and balances are designed to preserve the rights of the individual and the locality against preeminent central authority, you and I, Governors, recognize how dependent we both are, one upon the other, for the successful operation of our unique and happy form of government. Our system and our freedom permit the legislative to be pitted against the executive, the State against the Federal Government, the city against the countryside, party against party, interest against interest, all in competition or in contention one with another. Our task - your task in the State House and my task in the White House - is to weave from all these tangled threads a fabric of law and progress. We are not permitted the luxury of irresolution.

Others may confine themselves to debate, discussion, and that ultimate luxury - free advice. Our responsibility is one of decision - for to govern is to choose.

Thus, in a very real sense, you and I are the executors of the testament handed down by those who gathered in this historic hall 186 years ago today. For they gathered to affix their names to a document which was, above all else, a document not of rhetoric but of bold decision. It was, it is true, a document of protest - but protests had been made before. It set forth their grievances with eloquence - but such eloquence had been heard before. But what distinguished this paper from all the others was the final irrevocable decision that it took - to assert the independence of free States in place of colonies, and to commit to that goal their lives, their fortunes, and their sacred honor.

Today, 186 years later, that Declaration whose yellowing parchment and fading, almost illegible lines I saw in the past week in the National Archives in Washington is still a revolutionary document. To read it today is to hear a trumpet call. For that Declaration unleashed not merely a revolution against the British, but a revolution in human affairs. Its authors were highly conscious of its worldwide implications. And George Washington declared that liberty and self-government everywhere were, in his words, "finally staked on the experiment entrusted to the hands of the American people." This prophecy has been borne out. For 186 years this doctrine of national independence has shaken the globe - and it remains the most powerful force anywhere in the world today. There are those struggling to eke out a bare existence in a barren land who have never heard of free enterprise, but who cherish the idea of independence. There are those who are grappling with overpowering problems of illiteracy and ill health and who are ill-equipped to hold free elections. But they are determined to hold fast to their national independence. Even those unwilling or unable to take part in any struggle between East and West are strongly on the side of their own national independence.

If there is a single issue that divides the world today, it is independence - the independence of Berlin or Laos or Viet Nam; the longing for independence behind the Iron Curtain; the peaceful transition to independence in those newly emerging areas whose troubles some hope to exploit.

The theory of independence is as old as man himself, and it was not invented in this hall. But it was in this hall that the theory became a practice; that the word went out to all, in Thomas Jefferson's phrase, that "the God who gave us life, gave us liberty at the same time." And today this Nation - conceived in revolution, nurtured in liberty, maturing in independence - has no intention of abdicating its leadership in that worldwide movement for independence to any nation or society committed to systematic human oppression.

As apt and applicable as the Declaration of Independence is today, we would do well to honor that other historic document drafted in this hall - the Constitution of the United States. For it stressed not independence but interdependence - not the individual liberty of one but the indivisible liberty of all.

In most of the old colonial world, the struggle for independence is coming to an end. Even in areas behind the Curtain, that which Jefferson called "the disease of liberty" still appears to be infectious. With the passing of ancient empires, today less than 2 percent of the world's population lives in territories officially termed "dependent." As this effort for independence, inspired by the American Declaration of Independence, now approaches a successful close, a great new effort - for interdependence - is transforming the world about us.

And the spirit of that new effort is the same spirit which gave birth to the American Constitution.

That spirit is today most clearly seen across the Atlantic Ocean. The nations of Western Europe, long divided by feuds far more bitter than any which existed among the 13 colonies, are today joining together, seeking, as our forefathers sought, to find freedom in diversity and in unity, strength.

The United States looks on this vast new enterprise with hope and admiration. We do not regard a strong and united Europe as a rival but as a partner. To aid its progress has been the basic object of our foreign policy for 17 years. We believe that a united Europe will be capable of playing a greater role in the common defense, of responding more generously to the needs of poorer nations, of joining with the United States and others in lowering trade barriers, resolving problems of commerce, commodities, and currency, and developing coordinated policies in all economic, political, and diplomatic areas. We see in such a Europe a partner with whom we can deal on a basis of full equality in all the great and burdensome tasks of building and defending a community of free nations.

It would be premature at this time to do more than indicate the high regard with which we view the formation of this partnership. The first order of business is for our European friends to go forward in forming the more perfect union which will someday make this partnership possible.

A great new edifice is not built overnight. It was 11 years from the Declaration of Independence to the writing of the Constitution. The construction of workable federal institutions required still another generation. The greatest works of our Nation's founders lay not in documents and in declarations, but in creative, determined action. The building of the new house of Europe has followed the same practical, purposeful course. Building the Atlantic partnership now will not be easily or cheaply finished.

But I will say here and now, on this Day of Independence, that the United States will be ready for a Declaration of Interdependence, that we will be prepared to discuss with a united Europe the ways and means of forming a concrete Atlantic partnership, a mutually beneficial partnership between the new union now emerging in Europe and the old American Union founded here 175 years ago.

All this will not be completed in a year, but let the world know it is our goal.

In urging the adoption of the United States Constitution, Alexander Hamilton told his fellow New Yorkers "to think continentally." Today Americans must learn to think intercontinentally.

Acting on our own, by ourselves, we cannot establish justice throughout the world; we cannot insure its domestic tranquility, or provide for its common defense, or promote its general welfare, or secure the blessings of liberty to ourselves and our posterity. But joined with other free nations, we can do all this and more. We can assist the developing nations to throw off the yoke of poverty. We can balance our worldwide trade and payments at the highest possible level of growth. We can mount a deterrent powerful enough to deter any aggression. And ultimately we can help to achieve a world of law and free choice, banishing the world of war and coercion.

For the Atlantic partnership of which I speak would not look inward only, preoccupied with its own welfare and advancement. It must look outward to cooperate with all nations in meeting their common concern. It would serve as a nucleus for the eventual union of all free men - those who are now free and those who are vowing that some day they will be free.

On Washington's birthday in 1861, standing right there, President-elect Abraham Lincoln spoke in this hall on his way to the Nation's Capital. And he paid a brief but eloquent tribute to the men who wrote, who fought for, and who died for the Declaration of Independence. Its essence, he said, was its promise not only of liberty "to the people of this country, but hope to the world . . . [hope] that in due time the weights should be lifted from the shoulders of all men, and that all should have an equal chance."

On this fourth day of July, 1962, we who are gathered at this same hall, entrusted with the fate and future of our States and Nation, declare now our vow to do our part to lift the weights from the shoulders of all, to join other men and nations in preserving both peace and freedom, and to regard any threat to the peace or freedom of one as a threat to the peace and freedom of all. "And for the support of this Declaration, with a firm reliance on the protection of Divine Providence, we mutually pledge to each other our Lives, our Fortunes and our sacred Honor."

The Space Race
Rice University
Houston, Texas
September 12, 1962

I appreciate your president having made me an honorary visiting professor, and I will assure you that my first lecture will be very brief.

I am delighted to be here and I'm particularly delighted to be here on this occasion.

We meet at a college noted for knowledge, in a city noted for progress, in a State noted for strength, and we stand in need of all three, for we meet in an hour of change and challenge, in a decade of hope and fear, in an age of both knowledge and ignorance. The greater our knowledge increases, the greater our ignorance unfolds.

Despite the striking fact that most of the scientists that the world has ever known are alive and working today, despite the fact that this Nation's own scientific manpower is doubling every 12 years in a rate of growth more than three times that of our population as a whole, despite that, the vast stretches of the unknown and the unanswered and the unfinished still far outstrip our collective comprehension.

No man can fully grasp how far and how fast we have come, but condense, if you will, the 50,000 years of man's recorded history in a time span of but a half-century. Stated in these terms, we know very little about the first 40 years, except at the end of them advanced man had learned to use the skins of animals to cover them. Then about 10 years ago, under this standard, man emerged from his caves to construct other kinds of shelter. Only 5 years ago man learned to write and use a cart with wheels. Christianity began less than 2 years ago. The printing press came this year, and then less than 2 months ago, during this whole 50-year span of human history, the steam engine provided a new source of power.

Newton explored the meaning of gravity. Last month electric lights and telephones and automobiles and airplanes became available. Only last week did we develop penicillin and television and nuclear power, and now if America's new spacecraft succeeds in reaching Venus, we will have literally reached the stars before midnight tonight.

This is a breathtaking pace, and such a pace cannot help but create new ills as it dispels old, new ignorance, new problems, new dangers. Surely the opening vistas of space promise high costs and hardships, as well as high reward.

So it is not surprising that some would have us stay where we are a little longer to rest, to wait. But this city of Houston, this State of Texas, this country of the United States was not built by those who waited and rested and wished to look behind them. This country was conquered by those who moved forward - and so will space.

William Bradford, speaking in 1630 of the founding of the Plymouth Bay Colony, said that all great and honorable actions are accompanied with great difficulties, and both must be enterprised and overcome with answerable courage.

If this capsule history of our progress teaches us anything, it is that man, in his quest for knowledge and progress, is determined and cannot be deterred. The exploration of space will go ahead, whether we join in it or not, and it is one of the great adventures of all time, and no nation which expects to be the leader of other nations can expect to stay behind in this race for space.

Those who came before us made certain that this country rode the first waves of the industrial revolutions, the first waves of modern invention, and the first wave of nuclear power, and this generation does not intend to founder in the backwash of the coming age of space. We mean to be a part of it - we mean to lead it. For the eyes of the world now look into space, to the moon and to the planets beyond, and we have vowed that we shall not see it governed by a hostile flag of conquest, but by a banner of freedom and peace. We have vowed that we shall not see space filled with weapons of mass destruction, but with instruments of knowledge and understanding.

Yet the vows of this Nation can only be fulfilled if we in this Nation are first, and, therefore, we intend to be first. In short, our leadership in science and in industry, our hopes for peace and security, our obligations to ourselves as well as others, all require us to make this effort, to solve these mysteries, to solve them for the good of all men, and to become the world's leading space-faring nation.

We set sail on this new sea because there is new knowledge to be gained, and new rights to be won, and they must be won and used for the progress of all people. For space science, like nuclear science and all technology, has no conscience of its own. Whether it will become a force for good or ill depends on man, and only if the United States occupies a position of pre-eminence can we help decide whether this new ocean will be a sea of peace or a new terrifying theater of war. I do not say that we should or will go unprotected against the hostile misuse of space any more than we go unprotected against the hostile use of land or sea, but I do say that space can be explored and mastered without feeding the fires of war, without repeating the mistakes that man has made in extending his writ around this globe of ours.

There is no strife, no prejudice, no national conflict in outer space as yet. Its hazards are hostile to us all. Its conquest deserves the best of all mankind, and its opportunity for peaceful cooperation may never come again. But why, some say, the moon? Why choose this as our goal? And they may well ask why climb the highest mountain. Why, 35 years ago, fly the Atlantic? Why does Rice play Texas?

We choose to go to the moon. We choose to go to the moon in this decade and do the other things, not because they are easy, but because they are hard, because that goal will serve to organize and measure the best of our energies and skills, because that challenge is one that we are willing to accept, one we are unwilling to postpone, and one which we intend to win, and the others, too.

It is for these reasons that I regard the decision last year to shift our efforts in space from low to high gear as among the most important decisions that will be made during my incumbency in the Office of the Presidency.

In the last 24 hours we have seen facilities now being created for the greatest and most complex exploration in man's history. We have felt the ground shake and the air shattered by the testing of a Saturn C-1 booster rocket, many times as powerful as the Atlas which launched John Glenn, generating power equivalent to 10,000 automobiles with their accelerators on the floor. We have seen the site where five F-1 rocket engines, each one as powerful as all eight engines of the Saturn combined, will be clustered together to make the advanced Saturn missile, assembled in a new building to be built at Cape Canaveral as tall as a 48-story structure, as wide as a city block, and as long as two lengths of this field.

Within these last 19 months at least 45 satellites have circled the earth. Some 40 of them were "made in the United States of America" and they were far more sophisticated and supplied far more knowledge to the people of the world than those of the Soviet Union.

The Mariner spacecraft now on its way to Venus is the most intricate instrument in the history of space science. The accuracy of that shot is comparable to firing a missile from Cape Canaveral and dropping it in this stadium between the 40-yard lines.

Transit satellites are helping our ships at sea to steer a safer course. Tiros satellites have given us unprecedented warnings of hurricanes and storms, and will do the same for forest fires and icebergs.

We have had our failures, but so have others, even if they do not admit them. And they may be less public.

To be sure, we are behind, and will be behind for some time in manned flight. But we do not intend to stay behind, and in this decade we shall make up and move ahead.

The growth of our science and education will be enriched by new knowledge of our universe and environment, by new techniques of learning and mapping and observation, by new tools and computers for industry, medicine, the home as well as the school. Technical institutions, such as Rice, will reap the harvest of these gains.

And finally, the space effort itself, while still in its infancy, has already created a great number of new companies, and tens of thousands of new jobs. Space and related industries are generating new demands in investment and skilled personnel, and this city and this State, and this region, will share greatly in this growth. What was once the furthest outpost on the old frontier of the West will be the furthest outpost on the new frontier of science and space. Houston, your City of Houston, with its Manned Spacecraft Center, will become the heart of a large scientific and engineering community. During the next 5 years the National Aeronautics and Space Administration expects to double the number of scientists and engineers in this area, to increase its outlays for salaries and expenses to $60 million a year; to invest some $200 million in plant and laboratory facilities; and to direct or contract for new space efforts over $1 billion from this Center in this City.

To be sure, all this costs us all a good deal of money. This year's space budget is three times what it was in January 1961, and it is greater than the space budget of the previous 8 years combined. That budget now stands at $5,400 million a year - a staggering sum, though somewhat less than we pay for cigarettes and cigars every year. Space expenditures will soon rise some more, from 40 cents per person per week to more than 50 cents a week for every man, woman, and child in the United

States, for we have given this program a high national priority - even though I realize that this is in some measure an act of faith and vision, for we do not now know what benefits await us. But if I were to say, my fellow citizens, that we shall send to the moon, 240,000 miles away from the control station in Houston, a giant rocket more than 300 feet tall, the length of this football field, made of new metal alloys, some of which have not yet been invented, capable of standing heat and stresses several times more than have evere been experienced, fitted together with a precision better than the finest watch, carrying all the equipment needed for propulsion, guidance, control, communications, food and survival, on an untried mission, to an unknown celestial body, and then return it safely to earth, reentering the atmosphere at speeds of over 25,000 miles per hour, causing heat about half that of the temperature of the sun - almost as hot as it is here today - and do all this, and do it right, and do it first before this decade is out, then we must be bold.

I'm the one who is doing all the work, so we just want you to stay cool for a minute.

However, I think we're going to do it, and I think that we must pay what needs to be paid. I don't think we ought to waste any money, but I think we ought to do the job. And this will be done in the decade of the sixties. It may be done while some of you are still here at school at this college and university. It will be done during the terms of office of some of the people who sit here on this platform. But it will be done. And it will be done before the end of this decade.

I am delighted that this university is playing a part in putting a man on the moon as part of a great national effort of the United   States of America.

Many years ago the great British explorer George Mallory, who was to die on Mount Everest, was asked why did he want to climb it. He said, "Because it is there."

Well, space is there, and we're going to climb it, and the moon and the planets are there, and new hopes for knowledge and peace are there. And, therefore, as we set sail we ask God's blessing on the most hazardous and dangerous and greatest adventure on which man has ever embarked.

The Centennial of the
Emancipation Proclamation
Lincoln Memorial
Washington, DC
September 22, 1962

I take great pleasure in greeting you on this centennial commemoration of one of the most solemn moments in American history. One hundred years ago today Abraham Lincoln signed the Emancipation Proclamation. He thereby began the process which brought a final end to the evil of human slavery, which wiped out from our Nation what John Quincy Adams called the great stain upon the North American Union. But the Emancipation Proclamation was not an end. It was a beginning. The century since has seen the struggle to convert freedom from rhetoric to reality. It has been in many respects a somber story. For many years progress towards the realization of equal rights was very slow. A structure of segregation divided the Negro from his fellow American citizen. He was denied equal opportunity in education and employment. In many places he could not vote. For a long time he was exposed to violence and to terror. These were bitter years of humiliation and deprivation.

Looking back at this period, one must observe two remarkable facts. The first is that despite humiliation and deprivation, the Negro retained his loyalty to the United States and to democratic institutions. He showed this loyalty by brave service in two world wars, by the rejection of extreme or violent policies, by a quiet and proud determination to work for long-denied rights within the framework of the American Constitution.

The second is that despite humiliation and deprivation the Negro has never stopped working for his own salvation. There is no more impressive chapter in our history than the one in which our Negro fellow citizens sought better education for themselves and their children, built better schools and better houses, carved out their own economic opportunities, enlarged their press, fostered their arts, and clarified and strengthened their purpose as a people.

In doing these things, the Negroes enlisted the support of many of their fellow citizens both North and South. But the essential effort, the sustained struggle, was borne by the Negro alone with steadfast dignity and faith. And in due course the effort had its results. The last generation has seen a belated, but still spectacular, quickening of the pace of full emancipation. Twenty-five years ago the Nation would have been unbelieving at the progress to be made by the time of this centennial, progress in education, in employment, in the even-handed administration of justice, in access to the ballot, in the assumption of places of responsibility and leadership, in public and private life.

It has been a striking change, and a change wrought in large measure by the courage and perseverance of Negro men and women. It can be said, I believe, that Abraham Lincoln emancipated the slaves, but that in this century since, our Negro citizens have emancipated themselves.

And the task is not finished. Much remains to be done to eradicate the vestiges of discrimination and segregation, to make equal rights a reality for all of our people, to fulfill finally the promises of the Declaration of Independence. Like the proclamation we celebrate, this observance must be regarded not as an end, but a beginning. The best commemoration lies not in what we say today, but in what we do in the days and months ahead to complete the work begun by Abraham Lincoln a century ago. "In giving freedom to the slaves," President Lincoln said, "we assure freedom to the free." In giving rights to others which belong to them, we give rights to ourselves and to our country.

The Cuban Missile Crisis
Radio and Television Address
Washington, DC
October 22, 1962

This Government, as promised, has maintained the closest surveillance of the Soviet military buildup on the island of Cuba. Within the past week, unmistakable evidence has established the fact that a series of offensive missile sites is now in preparation on that imprisoned island. The purpose of these bases can be none other than to provide a nuclear strike capability against the Western Hemisphere.

Upon receiving the first preliminary hard information of this nature last Tuesday morning at 9 a.m., I directed that our surveillance be stepped up. And having now confirmed and completed our evaluation of the evidence and our decision on a course of action, this Government feels obliged to report this new crisis to you in fullest detail.

The characteristics of these new missile sites indicate two distinct types of installations. Several of them include medium range ballistic missiles, capable of carrying a nuclear warhead for a distance of more than 1,000 nautical miles. Each of these missiles, in short, is capable of striking Washington, D.C., the Panama Canal, Cape Canaveral, Mexico City, or any other city in the southeastern part of the United States, in Central America, or in the Caribbean area.

Additional sites not yet completed appear to be designed for intermediate range ballistic missiles - capable of traveling more than twice as far - and thus capable of striking most of the major cities in the Western

Hemisphere, ranging as far north as Hudson Bay, Canada, and as far south as Lima, Peru. In addition, jet bombers, capable of carrying nuclear weapons, are now being uncrated and assembled in Cuba, while the necessary air bases are being prepared.

This urgent transformation of Cuba into an important strategic base - by the presence of these large, long-range, and clearly offensive weapons of sudden mass destruction - constitutes an explicit threat to the peace and security of all the Americas, in flagrant and deliberate defiance of the Rio Pact of 1947, the traditions of this Nation and hemisphere, the joint resolution of the 87th Congress, the Charter of the United Nations, and my own public warnings to the Soviets on September 4 and 13. This action also contradicts the repeated assurances of Soviet spokesmen, both publicly and privately delivered, that the arms buildup in Cuba would retain its original defensive character, and that the Soviet Union had no need or desire to station strategic missiles on the territory of any other nation.

The size of this undertaking makes clear that it has been planned for some months. Yet only last month, after I had made clear the distinction between any introduction of ground-to-ground missiles and the existence of defensive antiaircraft missiles, the Soviet Government publicly stated on September 11 that, and I quote, "the armaments and military equipment sent to Cuba are designed exclusively for defensive purposes," that, and I quote the Soviet Government, "there is no need for the Soviet Government to shift its weapons . . . for a retaliatory blow to any other country, for instance Cuba," and that, and I quote their government, "the Soviet Union has so powerful rockets to carry these nuclear warheads that there is no need to search for sites for them beyond the boundaries of the Soviet Union." That statement was false.

Only last Thursday, as evidence of this rapid offensive buildup was already in my hand, Soviet Foreign Minister Gromyko told me in my office that he was instructed to make it clear once again, as he said his government had already done, that Soviet assistance to Cuba, and I quote, "pursued solely the purpose of contributing to the defense capabilities of Cuba," that, and I quote him, "training by Soviet specialists of Cuban nationals in handling defensive armaments was by no means offensive, and if it were otherwise," Mr. Gromyko went on, "the Soviet Government would never become involved in rendering such assistance." That statement also was false.

Neither the United States of America nor the world community of nations can tolerate deliberate deception and offensive threats on the part of any nation, large or small. We no longer live in a world where only the actual firing of weapons represents a sufficient challenge to a nation's security to constitute maximum peril. Nuclear weapons are so destructive and ballistic missiles are so swift, that any substantially increased possibility of their use or any sudden change in their deployment may well be regarded as a definite threat to peace.

For many years, both the Soviet Union and the United States, recognizing this fact, have deployed strategic nuclear weapons with great care, never upsetting the precarious status quo which insured that these weapons would not be used in the absence of some vital challenge. Our own strategic missiles have never been transferred to the territory of any other nation under a cloak of secrecy and deception; and our history - unlike that of the Soviets since the end of World War II - demonstrates that we have no desire to dominate or conquer any other nation or impose our system upon its people. Nevertheless, American citizens have become adjusted to living daily on the bull's-eye of Soviet missiles located inside the U.S.S.R. or in submarines.

In that sense, missiles in Cuba add to an already clear and present danger - although it should be noted the nations of Latin America have never previously been subjected to a potential nuclear threat.

But this secret, swift, and extraordinary buildup of Communist missiles - in an area well known to have a special and historical relationship to the United States and the nations of the Western Hemisphere, in violation of Soviet assurances, and in defiance of American and hemispheric policy - this sudden, clandestine decision to station strategic weapons for the first time outside of Soviet soil - is a deliberately provocative and unjustified change in the status quo which cannot be accepted by this country, if our courage and our commitments are ever to be trusted again by either friend or foe.

The 1930's taught us a clear lesson: aggressive conduct, if allowed to go unchecked and unchallenged, ultimately leads to war. This nation is opposed to war. We are also true to our word. Our unswerving objective, therefore, must be to prevent the use of these missiles against this or any other country, and to secure their withdrawal or elimination from the Western Hemisphere.

Our policy has been one of patience and restraint, as befits a peaceful and powerful nation, which leads a worldwide alliance. We have been determined not to be diverted from our central concerns by mere irritants and fanatics. But now further action is required - and it is under way; and these actions may only be the beginning. We will not prematurely or unnecessarily risk the costs of worldwide nuclear war in which even the fruits of victory would be ashes in our mouth - but neither will we shrink from that risk at any time it must be faced.

Acting, therefore, in the defense of our own security and of the entire Western Hemisphere, and under the authority entrusted to me by the Constitution as endorsed by the resolution of the Congress, I have directed that the following *initial* steps be taken immediately:

First To halt this offensive buildup, a strict quarantine on all offensive military equipment under shipment to Cuba is being initiated. All ships of any kind bound for Cuba from whatever nation or port will, if found to contain cargoes of offensive weapons, be turned back. This quarantine will be extended, if needed, to other types of cargo and carriers. We are not at this time, however, denying the necessities of life as the Soviets attempted to do in their Berlin blockade of 1948.

Second I have directed the continued and increased close surveillance of Cuba and its military buildup. The foreign ministers of the OAS, in their communique of October 6, rejected secrecy on such matters in this hemisphere. Should these offensive military preparations continue, thus increasing the threat to the hemisphere, further action will be justified. I have directed the Armed Forces to prepare for any eventualities; and I trust that in the interest of both the Cuban people and the

Soviet technicians at the sites, the hazards to all concerned of continuing this threat will be recognized.

Third. It shall be the policy of this Nation to regard any nuclear missile launched from Cuba against any nation in the Western Hemisphere as an attack by the Soviet Union on the United States, requiring a full retaliatory response upon the Soviet Union.

Fourth. As a necessary military precaution, I have reinforced our base at Guantanamo, evacuated today the dependents of our personnel there, and ordered additional military units to be on a stand by alert basis.

Fifth. We are calling tonight for an immediate meeting of the Organ of Consultation under the Organization of American States, to consider this threat to hemispheric security and to invoke articles 6 and 8 of the Rio Treaty in support of all necessary action. The United Nations Charter allows for regional security arrangements - and the nations of this hemisphere decided long ago against the military presence of outside powers. Our other allies around the world have also been alerted.

Sixth. Under the Charter of the United Nations, we are asking tonight that an emergency meeting of the Security Council be convoked without delay to take action against this latest Soviet threat to world peace. Our resolution will call for the prompt dismantling and withdrawal of all offensive weapons in Cuba, under the supervision of U.N. observers, before the quarantine can be lifted.

Seventh and finally. I call upon Chairman Khrushchev to halt and eliminate this clandestine, reckless, and provocative threat to world peace and to stable relations between our two nations. I call upon him further to abandon this course of world domination, and to join in an historic effort to end the perilous arms race and to transform the history of man. He has an opportunity now to move the world back from the abyss of destruction - by returning to his government's own words that it had no need to station missiles outside its own territory, and withdrawing these weapons from Cuba - by refraining from any action which will widen or deepen the present crisis - and then by participating in a search for peaceful and permanent solutions.

This Nation is prepared to present its case against the Soviet threat to peace, and our own proposals for a peaceful world, at any time and in any forum - in the OAS, in the United Nations, or in any other meeting that could be useful - without limiting our freedom of action. We have in the past made strenuous efforts to limit the spread of nuclear weapons. We have proposed the elimination of all arms and military bases in a fair and effective disarmament treaty. We are prepared to discuss new proposals for the removal of tensions on both sides - including the possibilities of a genuinely independent Cuba, free to determine its own destiny. We have no wish to war with the Soviet Union - for we are a peaceful people who desire to live in peace with all other peoples.

But it is difficult to settle or even discuss these problems in an atmosphere of intimidation. That is why this latest Soviet threat - or any other threat which is made either independently or in response to our actions this week - must and will be met with determination. Any hostile move anywhere in the world against the safety and freedom of peoples to whom we are committed -

including in particular the brave people of West Berlin - will be met by whatever action is needed.

Finally, I want to say a few words to the captive people of Cuba, to whom this speech is being directly carried by special radio facilities. I speak to you as a friend, as one who knows of your deep attachment to your fatherland, as one who shares your aspirations for liberty and justice for all. And I have watched, and the American people have watched, with deep sorrow how your nationalist revolution was betrayed - and how your fatherland fell under foreign domination. Now your leaders are no longer Cuban leaders inspired by Cuban ideals. They are puppets and agents of an international conspiracy which has turned Cuba against your friends and neighbors in the Americas - and turned it into the first Latin American country to become a target for nuclear war - the first Latin American country to have these weapons on its soil.

These new weapons are not in your interest. They contribute nothing to your peace and well-being. They can only undermine it. But this country has no wish to cause you to suffer or to impose any system upon you. We know that your lives and land are being used as pawns by those who deny your freedom.

Many times in the past, the Cuban people have risen to throw out tyrants who destroyed their liberty. And I have no doubt that most Cubans today look forward to the time when they will be truly free - free from foreign domination, free to choose their own leaders, free to select their own system, free to own their own land, free to speak and write and worship without fear or degradation. And then shall Cuba be welcomed back to the society of free nations and to the associations of this hemisphere.

My fellow citizens: let no one doubt that this is a difficult and dangerous effort on which we have set out. No one can foresee precisely what course it will take or what costs or casualties will be incurred. Many months of sacrifice and self-discipline lie ahead - months in which both our patience and our will will be tested - months in which many threats and denunciations will keep us aware of our dangers. But the greatest danger of all would be to do nothing.

The path we have chosen for the present is full of hazards, as all paths are - but it is the one most consistent with our character and courage as a nation and our commitments around the world. The cost of freedom is always high - but Americans have always paid it. And one path we shall never choose, and that is the path of surrender or submission.

Our goal is not the victory of might, but the vindication of right - not peace at the expense of freedom, but peace *and* freedom, here in this hemisphere, and, we hope, around the world. God willing, that goal will be achieved.

The State of the Union
Washington, DC
January 14, 1963

I congratulate you all - not merely on your electoral victory but on your selected role in history. For you and I are privileged to serve the great Republic in what could be the most decisive decade in its long history. The choices we make, for good or ill, may well shape the state of the Union for generations yet to come.

Little more than 100 weeks ago I assumed the office of President of the United States. In seeking the help of the Congress and our countrymen, I pledged no easy answers. I pledged - and asked - only toil and dedication. These the Congress and the people have given in good measure. And today, having witnessed in recent months a heightened respect for our national purpose and power - having seen the courageous calm of a united people in a perilous hour - and having observed a steady improvement in the opportunities and well-being of our citizens - I can report to you that the state of this old but youthful Union, in the 175th year of its life, is good.

In the world beyond our borders, steady progress has been made in building a world of order. The people of West Berlin remain both free and secure. A settlement, though still precarious, has been reached in Laos. The spearpoint of aggression has been blunted in Viet Nam. The end of agony may be in sight in the Congo. The doctrine of troika is dead. And, while danger continues, a deadly threat has been removed in Cuba.

At home, the recession is behind us. Well over a million more men and women are working today than were working 2 years ago. The average factory workweek is once again more than 40 hours; our industries are turning out more goods than ever before; and more than half of the manufacturing capacity that lay silent and wasted 100 weeks ago is humming with activity.

In short, both at home and abroad, there may now be a temptation to relax. For the road has been long, the burden heavy, and the pace consistently urgent.

But we cannot be satisfied to rest here. This is the side of the hill, not the top. The mere absence of war is not peace. The mere absence of recession is not growth. We have made a beginning - but we have only begun.

Now the time has come to make the most of our gains to translate the renewal of our national strength into the achievement of our national purpose.

America has enjoyed 22 months of uninterrupted economic recovery. But recovery is not enough. If we are to prevail in the long run, we must expand the long-run strength of our economy. We must move along the path to a higher rate of growth and full employment.

For this would mean tens of billions of dollars more each year in production, profits, wages, and public revenues. It would mean an end to the persistent slack which has kept our unemployment at or above 5 percent for 61 out of the past 62 months - and an end to the growing pressures for such restrictive measures as the 35-hour week, which alone could increase hourly labor costs by as much as 14 percent, start a new wage-price spiral of inflation, and undercut our efforts to compete with other nations.

To achieve these greater gains, one step, above all, is essential - the enactment this year of a substantial reduction and revision in Federal income taxes.

For it is increasingly clear - to those in Government, business, and labor who are responsible for our economy's success - that our obsolete tax system exerts too heavy a drag on private purchasing power, profits, and employment. Designed to check inflation in earlier years, it now checks growth instead. It discourages extra effort and risk. It distorts the use of resources. It invites recurrent recessions, depresses our Federal revenues, and causes chronic budget deficits.

Now, when the inflationary pressures of the war and the post-war years no longer threaten, and the dollar commands new respect - now, when no military crisis strains our resources - now is the time to act. We cannot afford to be timid or slow. For this is the most urgent task confronting the Congress in 1963.

In an early message, I shall propose a permanent reduction in tax rates which will lower liabilities by $13.5 billion. Of this, $11 billion results from reducing individual tax rates, which now range between 20 and 91 percent, to a more sensible range of 14 to 65 percent, with a split in the present first bracket. Two and one-half billion dollars results from reducing corporate tax rates, from 52 percent - which gives the Government today a majority interest in profits - to the permanent pre-Korean level of 47 percent. This is in addition to the more than $2 billion cut in corporate tax liabilities resulting from last year's investment credit and depreciation reform.

To achieve this reduction within the limits of a manageable budgetary deficit, I urge: first, that these cuts be phased over 3 calendar years, beginning in 1963 with a cut of some $6 billion at annual rates; second, that these reductions be coupled with selected structural changes, beginning in 1964, which will broaden the tax base, end unfair or unnecessary preferences, remove or lighten certain hardships, and in the net offset some $3.5 billion of the revenue loss; and third, that budgetary receipts at the outset be increased by $1.5 billion a year, without any change in tax liabilities, by gradually shifting the tax payments of large corporations to a more current time schedule. This combined program, by increasing the amount of our national income, will in time result in still higher Federal revenues. It is a fiscally responsible program - the surest and the soundest way of achieving in time a balanced budget in a balanced, full employment economy.

This net reduction in tax liabilities of $10 billion will increase the purchasing power of American families and business enterprises in every tax bracket, with greatest increase going to our low-income consumers. It will, in addition, encourage the initiative and risk-taking on which our free system depends - induce more investment, production, and capacity use - help provide the 2 million new jobs we need every year - and reinforce the American principle of additional reward for additional effort.

I do not say that a measure for tax reduction and reform is the only way to achieve these goals.

No doubt a massive increase in Federal spending could also create jobs and growth - but, in today's setting, private consumers, employers, and investors should be given a full opportunity first.

No doubt a temporary tax cut could provide a spur to our economy - but a long-run problem compels a long-run solution.

No doubt a reduction in either individual or corporation taxes alone would be of great help - but corporations need customers and job seekers need jobs.

No doubt tax reduction without reform would sound simpler and more attractive to many - but our growth is also hampered by a host of tax inequities and special preferences which have distorted the flow of investment.

And, finally there are no doubt some who would prefer to put off a tax cut in the hope that ultimately an end to the cold war would make possible an equivalent cut in expenditures - but that end is not in view and to wait for it would be costly and self-defeating.

In submitting a tax program which will, of course, temporarily increase the deficit but can ultimately end it, and, in recognition of the need to control expenditures, I will shortly submit a fiscal 1964 administrative budget which, while allowing for needed rises in defense, space, and fixed interest charges, holds total expenditures for all other purposes below this year's level.

This requires the reduction or postponement of many desirable programs, the absorption of a large part of last year's Federal pay raise through personnel and other economies, the termination of certain installations and projects, and the substitution in several programs of private for public credit. But I am convinced that the enactment this year of tax reduction and tax reform overshadows all other domestic problems in this Congress. For we cannot for long lead the cause of peace and freedom, if we ever cease to set the pace here at home.

Tax reduction alone, however, is not enough to strengthen our society, to provide opportunities for the four million Americans who are born every year, to improve the lives of 32 million Americans who live on the outskirts of poverty.

The quality of American life must keep pace with the quantity of American goods.

This country cannot afford to be materially rich and spiritually poor.

Therefore, by holding down the budgetary cost of existing programs to keep within the limitations I have set, it is both possible and imperative to adopt other new measure that we cannot afford to postpone.

These measures are based on a series of fundamental premises, grouped under four related headings:

First, we need to strengthen our Nation by investing in our youth:

The future of any country which is dependent upon the will and wisdom of its citizens is damaged, and irreparably damaged, whenever any of its children is not educated to the full extent of his talent, from grade school through graduate school. Today, an estimated 4 out of every 10 students in the 5th grade will not even finish high school - and that is a waste we cannot afford.

In addition, there is no reason why one million young Americans, out of school and out of work, should all remain unwanted and often untrained on our city streets when their energies can be put to good use.

Finally, the overseas success of our Peace Corps volunteers, most of them young men and women carrying skills and ideas to needy people, suggests the merit of a similar corps serving our own community needs: in mental hospitals, on Indian reservations, in centers for the aged or for young delinquents, in schools for the illiterate or the handicapped. As the idealism of our youth has served world peace, so can it serve the domestic tranquility.

Second, we need to strengthen our Nation by safeguarding its health:

Our working men and women, instead of being forced to beg for help from public charity once they are old and ill, should start contributing now to their own retirement health program through the Social Security System.

Moreover, all our miracles of medical research will count for little if we cannot reverse the growing nationwide shortage of doctors, dentists, and nurses, and the widespread shortages of nursing homes and modern urban hospital facilities. Merely to keep the present ratio of doctors and dentists from declining any further, we must over the next 10 years increase the capacity of our medical schools by 50 percent and our dental schools by 100 percent.

Finally, and of deep concern, I believe that the abandonment of the mentally ill and the mentally retarded to the grim mercy of custodial institutions too often inflicts on them and on their families a needless cruelty which this Nation should not endure. The incidence of mental retardation in this country is three times as high as that of Sweden, for example - and that figure can and must be reduced.

Third, we need to strengthen our Nation by protecting the basic rights of its citizens:

The right to competent counsel must be assured to every man accused of crime in Federal court, regardless of his means.

And the most precious and powerful right in the world, the right to vote in a free American election, must not be denied to any citizen on grounds of his race or color. I wish that all qualified Americans permitted to vote were willing to vote, but surely in this centennial year of Emancipation all those who are willing to vote should always be permitted.

Fourth, we need to strengthen our Nation by making the best and the most economical use of its resources and facilities:

Our economic health depends on healthy transportation arteries; and I believe the way to a more modern, economical choice of national transportation service is through increased competition and decreased regulation. Local mass transit, faring even worse, is as essential a community service as hospitals and highways. Nearly three fourths of our citizens live in urban areas, which occupy only 2 percent of our land - and if local transit is to survive and relieve the congestion of these cities, it needs Federal stimulation and assistance.

Next, this Government is in the storage and stockpile business to the melancholy tune of more than $16 billion. We must continue to support farm income, but we should not pile more farm surpluses on top of the $7.5 billion we already own. We must maintain a stockpile of strategic materials, but the $8.5 billion we have acquired - for reasons both good and bad - is much more than we need; and we should be empowered to dispose of the excess in ways which will not cause market disruption.

Finally, our already overcrowded national parks and recreation areas will have twice as many visitors 10 years from now as they do today. If we do not plan today for the future growth of these and other great natural assets - not only parks and forests, but wildlife and wilderness preserves, and water projects of all kinds - our children and their children will be poorer in every sense of the word.

These are not domestic concerns alone.   For upon our achievement of greater vitality and strength here at home hang our fate and future in the world: our ability to sustain and supply the security of free men and nations, our ability to command their respect for our leadership, our ability to expand our trade without threat to our balance of payments, and our ability to adjust to the changing demands of cold war competition and challenge.

We shall be judged more by what we do at home than by what we preach abroad. Nothing we could do to help the developing countries would help them half as much as a booming U.S. economy. And nothing our opponents could do to encourage their own ambitions would encourage them half as much as a chronic lagging U.S. economy. These domestic tasks do not divert energy from our security - they provide the very foundation for freedom's survival and success.

Turning to the world outside, it was only a few years ago - in Southeast Asia, Africa, Eastern Europe, Latin America, even outer space - that communism sought to convey the image of a unified, confident, and expanding empire, closing in on a sluggish America and a free world in disarray. But few people would hold to that picture today.

In these past months we have reaffirmed the scientific and military superiority of freedom. We have doubled our efforts in space, to assure us of being first in the future. We have undertaken the most far-reaching defense improvements in the peacetime history of this country. And we have maintained the frontiers of freedom from Viet Nam to West Berlin.

But complacency or self-congratulation can imperil our security as much as the weapons of tyranny. A moment of pause is not a promise of peace. Dangerous problems remain from Cuba to the South China Sea. The world's prognosis prescribes, in short, not a year's vacation for us, but a year of obligation and opportunity.

Four special avenues of opportunity stand out: the Atlantic Alliance, the developing nations, the new Sino-Soviet difficulties, and the search for worldwide peace.

First, how fares the grand alliance? Free Europe is entering into a new phase of its long and brilliant history. The era of colonial expansion has passed; the era of national rivalries is fading; and a new era of interdependence and unity is taking shape. Defying the old prophecies of Marx, consenting to what no conqueror could ever compel, the free nations of Europe are moving toward a unity of purpose and power and policy in every sphere of activity.

For 17 years this movement has had our consistent support, both political and economic. Far from resenting the new Europe, we regard her as a welcome partner, not a rival. For the road to world peace and freedom is still long, and there are burdens which only full partners can share - in supporting the common defense, in expanding world trade, in aligning our balance of payments, in aiding the emergent nations, in concerting political and economic policies, and in welcoming to our common effort other industrialized nations, notably Japan, whose remarkable economic and political development of the 1950's permits it now to play on the world scene a major constructive role.

No doubt differences of opinion will continue to get more attention than agreements on action, as Europe moves from independence to more formal interdependence. But these are honest differences among honorable associates - more real and frequent, in fact, among our Western European allies than between them and the United States. For the unity of freedom has never relied on uniformity of opinion. But the basic agreement of this alliance on fundamental issues continues.

The first task of the alliance remains the common defense. Last month Prime Minister Macmillan and I laid plans for a new stage in our long cooperative effort, one which aims to assist in the wider task of framing a common nuclear defense for the whole alliance.

The Nassau agreement recognizes that the security of the West is indivisible, and so must be our defense. But it also recognizes that this is an alliance of proud and sovereign nations, and works best when we do not forget it. It recognizes further that the nuclear defense of the West is not a matter for the present nuclear powers alone - that France will be such a power in the future - and that ways must be found without increasing the hazards of nuclear diffusion, to increase the role of our other partners in planning, manning, and directing a truly multilateral nuclear force within an increasingly intimate NATO alliance. Finally, the Nassau agreement recognizes that nuclear defense is not enough, that the agreed NATO levels of conventional strength must be met, and that the alliance cannot afford to be in a position of having to answer every threat with nuclear weapons or nothing.

We remain too near the Nassau decisions, and too far from their full realization, to know their place in history. But I believe that, for the first time, the door is open for the nuclear defense of the alliance to become a source of confidence, instead of a cause of contention.

The next most pressing concern of the alliance is our common economic goals of trade and growth. This Nation continuous to be concerned about its balances-of-payments deficit, which, despite its decline, remains a stubborn and troublesome problem. We believe, moreover, that closer economic ties among all free nations are essential to prosperity and peace. And neither we nor the members of the European Common Market are so affluent that we can long afford to shelter high cost farms or factories from the winds of foreign competition, or to restrict the channels of trade with other nations of the free world. If the Common Market should move toward protectionism and restrictionism, it would undermine its own basic principles. This Government means to use the authority conferred on it last year by the Congress to encourage trade expansion on both sides of the Atlantic and around the world.

Second, what of the developing and non-aligned nations? They were shocked by the Soviets' sudden and secret attempt to transform Cuba into a nuclear striking base and by Communist China's arrogant invasion of India. They have been reassured by our prompt assistance to India, by our support through the United Nations of the Congo's unification, by our patient search for disarmament, and by the improvement in our treatment of citizens and visitors whose skins do not happen to be white. And as the older colonialism recedes, and the neo-colonialism of the Communist powers stands out more starkly than ever, they realize more clearly that the issue in the world struggle is not communism versus capitalism, but coercion versus free choice.

They are beginning to realize that the longing for independence is the same the world over, whether it is the independence of West Berlin or Viet Nam. They are beginning to realize that such independence runs athwart all Communist ambitions but is in keeping with our own - and that our approach to their diverse needs is resilient and resourceful, while the Communists are still relying on ancient doctrines and dogmas.

Nevertheless it is hard for any nation to focus on an external or subversive threat to its independence when its energies are drained in daily combat with the forces of poverty and despair. It makes little sense for us to assail, in speeches and resolutions, the horrors of communism, to spend $50 billion a year to prevent its military advance - and then to begrudge spending, largely on American products, less than one-tenth of that amount, to help other nations strengthen their independence and cure the social chaos in which communism always has thrived.

I am proud - and I think most Americans are proud - of a mutual defense and assistance program, evolved with bipartisan support in three administrations, which has, with all its recognized problems, contributed to the fact that not a single one of the nearly fifty U.N. members to gain independence since the Second World War has succumbed to Communist control.

I am proud of a program that has helped to arm and feed and clothe millions of people who live on the front lines of freedom.

I am especially proud that this country has put forward for the 60's a vast cooperative effort to achieve economic growth and social progress throughout the Americas - the Alliance for Progress.

I do not underestimate the difficulties that we face in this mutual effort among our close neighbors, but the free states of this hemisphere, working in close collaboration, have begun to make this alliance a living reality. Today it is feeding one out of every four school age children in Latin America an extra food ration from our farm surplus. It has distributed 1.5 million school books and is building 17,000 classrooms. It has helped resettle tens of thousand of farm families on land they can call their own. It is stimulating our good neighbors to more self-help and self-reform - fiscal, social, institutional, and land reforms. It is bringing new housing and hope, new health and dignity, to millions who were forgotten. The men and women of this hemisphere know that the alliance cannot succeed if it is only another name for United States handouts - that it can succeed only as the Latin American nations themselves devote their best effort to fulfilling its goals.

This story is the same in Africa, in the Middle East, and in Asia. Wherever nations are willing to help themselves, we stand ready to help them build new bulwarks of freedom. We are not purchasing votes for the cold war; we have gone to the aid of imperiled nations, neutrals and allies alike. What we do ask - and all that we ask - is that our help be used to best advantage, and that their own efforts not be diverted by needless quarrels with other independent nations.

Despite all its past achievements, the continued progress of the mutual assistance program requires a persistent discontent with present performance. We have been reorganizing this program to make it a more effective, efficient instrument - and that process will continue this year.

But free world development will still be an uphill struggle. Government aid can only supplement the role of private investment, trade expansion, commodity stabilization, and, above all, internal self-improvement. The processes of growth are gradual - bearing fruit in a decade, not a day. Our successes will be neither quick nor dramatic. But if these programs were ever to be ended, our failures in a dozen countries would be sudden and certain.

Neither money nor technical assistance, however, can be our only weapon against poverty. In the end, the crucial effort is one of purpose, requiring the fuel of finance but also a torch of idealism. And nothing carries the spirit of this American idealism more effectively to the far corners of the earth than the American Peace Corps.

A year ago, less than 900 Peace Corps volunteers were on the job. A year from now they will number more than 9,000 - men and women aged 18 to 79, willing to give 2 years of their lives to helping people in other lands.

There are, in fact, nearly a million Americans serving their country and the cause of freedom in overseas posts, a record no other people can match. Surely those of us who stay at home should be glad to help indirectly: by supporting our aid programs; by opening our doors to foreign visitors and diplomats and students; and by proving, day by day, by deed as well as word, that we are a just and generous people.

Third, what comfort can we take from the increasing strains and tensions within the Communist bloc? Here hope must be tempered with caution. For the Soviet-Chinese disagreement is over means, not ends. A dispute over how best to bury the free world is no grounds for Western rejoicing.

Nevertheless, while a strain is not a fracture, it is clear that the forces of diversity are at work inside the Communist camp, despite all the iron disciplines of regimentation and all the iron dogmatisms of ideology. Marx is proven wrong once again: for it is the closed Communist societies, not the free and open societies which carry within themselves the seeds of internal disintegration.

The disarray of the Communist empire has been heightened by two other formidable forces. One is the historical force of nationalism - and the yearning of all men to be free. The other is the gross inefficiency of their economies. For a closed society is not open to ideas of progress - and a police state finds that it cannot command the grain to grow.

New nations asked to choose between two competing systems need only compare conditions in East and West Germany, Eastern and Western Europe, North and South Viet Nam. They need only compare the disillusionment of Communist Cuba with the promise of the Alliance for Progress. And all the world knows that no successful system builds a wall to keep its people in and freedom out - and the wall of shame dividing Berlin is a symbol of Communist failure.

Finally, what can we do to move from the present pause toward enduring peace? Again I would counsel caution. I foresee no spectacular reversal in Communist methods or goals. But if all these trends and developments can persuade the Soviet Union to walk the path of peace, then let her know that all free nations will journey with her. But until that choice is made, and until the world can develop a reliable system of international security, the free peoples have no choice but to keep their arms nearby.

This country, therefore, continues to require the best defense in the world - a defense which is suited to the sixties. This means, unfortunately, a rising defense budget - for there is no substitute for adequate defense, and no "bargain basement" way of achieving it. It means the expenditure of more than $15 billion this year on nuclear weapons systems alone, a sum which is about equal to the combined defense budgets of our European Allies.

But it also means improved air and missile defenses, improved civil defense, a strengthened anti-guerilla capacity and, of prime importance, more powerful and flexible non-nuclear forces. For threats of massive retaliation may not deter piecemeal aggression - and a line of destroyers in a quarantine, or a division of well-equipped men on a border, may be more useful to our real security than the multiplication of awesome weapons beyond all rational need.

But our commitment to national safety is not a commitment to expand our military establishment indefinitely. We do not dismiss disarmament as merely an idle dream. For we believe that, in the end, it is the only way to assure the security of all without impairing the interests of any. Nor do we mistake honorable negotiation for appeasement. While we shall never weary in the defense of freedom, neither shall we ever abandon the pursuit of peace.

In this quest, the United Nations requires our full and continued support. Its value in serving the cause of peace has been shown anew in its role in the West New Guinea settlement, in its use as a forum for the Cuban crisis, and in its task of unification in the Congo. Today the United Nations is primarily the protector of the small and the weak, and a safety valve for the strong. Tomorrow it can form the framework for a world of law - a world in which no nation dictates the destiny of another, and in which the vast resources now devoted to destructive means will serve constructive ends.

In short, let our adversaries choose. If they choose peaceful competition, they shall have it. If they come to realize that their ambitions cannot succeed - if they see their "wars of liberation" and subversion will ultimately fail - if they recognize that there is more security in accepting inspection than in permitting new nations to master the black arts of nuclear war - and if they are willing to turn their energies, as we are, to the great unfinished tasks of our own peoples - then, surely, the areas of agreement can be very wide indeed: a clear understanding about Berlin, stability in Southeast Asia, an end to nuclear testing, new checks on surprise or accidental attack, and, ultimately, general and complete disarmament.

For we seek not the worldwide victory of one nation or system but a worldwide victory of man. The modern globe is too small, its weapons are too destructive, and its disorders are too contagious to permit any other kind of victory.

To achieve this end, the United States will continue to spend a greater portion of its national production than any other people in the free world. For 15 years no other free nation has demanded so much of itself. Through hot wars and cold, through recession and prosperity, through the ages of the atom and outer space, the American people have never faltered and their faith has never flagged. If at times our actions seem to make life difficult for others, it is only because history has made life difficult for us all.

But difficult days need not be dark. I think these are proud and memorable days in the cause of peace and freedom. We are proud, for example, of Major Rudolf Anderson, who gave his life over the island of Cuba. We salute Specialist James Allen Johnson, who died on the border of South Korea. We pay honor to Sergeant Gerald Pendall, who was killed in Viet Nam. They are among the many who in this century, far from home, have died for our country. Our task now, and the task of all Americans is to live up to their commitment.

My friends: I close on a note of hope. We are not lulled by the momentary calm of the sea or the somewhat clearer skies above. We know the turbulence that lies below, and the storms that are beyond the horizon this year. But now the winds of change appear to be blowing more strongly than ever, in the world of communism as well as our own. For 175 years we have sailed with those winds at our back, and with the tides of human freedom in our favor. We steer our ship with hope, as Thomas Jefferson said, "leaving Fear astern."

Today we still welcome those winds of change - and we have every reason to believe that our tide is running strong. With thanks to Almighty God for seeing us through a perilous passage, we ask His help anew in guiding the "Good Ship Union."

Civil Rights Message
Washington, DC
February 28, 1963

To the Congress of the United States:

"Our Constitution is color blind," wrote Mr. Justice Harlan before the turn of the century, "and neither knows nor tolerates classes among citizens." But the practices of the country do not always conform to the principles of the Constitution. And this Message is intended to examine how far we have come in achieving first-class citizenship for all citizens regardless of color, how far we have yet to go, and what further tasks remain to be carried out - by the Executive and Legislative Branches of the Federal Government, as well as by state and local governments and private citizens and organizations.

One hundred years ago the Emancipation Proclamation was signed by a President who believed in the equal worth and opportunity of every human being. That Proclamation was only a first step - a step which its author unhappily did not live to follow up, a step which some of its critics dismissed as an action which "frees the slave but ignores the Negro." Through these long one hundred years, while slavery has vanished, progress for the Negro has been too often blocked and delayed. Equality before the law has not always meant equal treatment and opportunity. And the harmful, wasteful and wrongful results of racial discrimination and segregation still appear in virtually every aspect of national life, in virtually every part of the Nation.

The Negro baby born in America today - regardless of the section or state in which he is born - has about one-half as much chance of completing high school as a white baby born in the same place on the same day - one-third as much chance of completing college - one-third as much chance of becoming a professional man - twice as much chance of becoming unemployed - about one-seventh as much chance of earning $10,000 per year - a life expectancy which is seven years less - and the prospects of earning only half as much.

No American who believes in the basic truth that "all men are created equal, that they are endowed by their Creator with certain unalienable Rights", can fully excuse, explain or defend the picture these statistics portray. Race discrimination hampers our economic growth by preventing the maximum development and utilization of our manpower. It hampers our world leadership by contradicting at home the message we preach abroad. It mars the atmosphere of a united and classless society in which this Nation rose to greatness. It increases the costs of public welfare, crime, delinquency and disorder. Above all, it is wrong.

Therefore, let it be clear, in our own hearts and minds, that it is not merely because of the Cold War, and not merely because of the economic waste of discrimination, that we are committed to achieving true equality of opportunity. The basic reason is because it is right.

The cruel disease of discrimination knows no sectional or state boundaries. The continuing attack on this problem must be equally broad. It must be both private and public - it must be conducted at national, state and local levels - and it must include both legislative and executive action.

In the last two years, more progress has been made in securing the civil rights of all Americans than in any comparable period in our history. Progress has been made - through executive action, litigation, persuasion and private initiative - in achieving and protecting equality of opportunity in education, voting, transportation, employment, housing, government, and the enjoyment of public accommodations.

But pride in our progress must not give way to relaxation of our effort. Nor does progress in the Executive Branch enable the Legislative Branch to escape its own obligations. On the contrary, it is in the light of this nationwide progress, and in the belief that Congress will wish once again to meet its responsibilities in this matter, that I stress in the following agenda of existing and prospective action important legislative as well as administrative measures.

The right to vote in a free American election is the most powerful and precious right in the world - and it must not be denied on the grounds of race or color. It is a potent key to achieving other rights of citizenship. For American history - both recent and past - clearly reveals that the power of the ballot has enabled those who achieve it to win other achievements as well, to gain a full voice in the affairs of their state and nation, and to see their interests represented in the governmental bodies which affect their future. In a free society, those with the power to govern are necessarily responsive to those with the right to vote.

In enacting the 1957 and 1960 Civil Rights Acts, Congress provided the Department of Justice with basic tools for protecting the right to vote - and this

Administration has not hesitated to use those tools. Legal action is brought only after voluntary efforts fail - and, in scores of instances, local officials, at the request of the Department of Justice, have voluntarily made voting records available or abandoned discriminatory registration, discriminatory voting practices or segregated balloting. Where voluntary local compliance has not been forthcoming, the Department of Justice has approximately quadrupled the previous level of its legal effort - investigating coercion, inspecting records, initiating lawsuits, enjoining intimidation, and taking whatever follow-up action is necessary to forbid further interference or discrimination. As a result, thousands of Negro citizens are registering and voting for the first time - many of them in counties where no Negro had ever voted before. The Department of Justice will continue to take whatever action is required to secure the right to vote for all Americans.

Experience has shown, however, that these highly useful Acts of the 85th and 86th Congresses suffer from two major defects. One is the usual long and difficult delay which occurs between the filing of a lawsuit and its ultimate conclusion. In one recent case, for example, nineteen months elapsed between the filing of the suit and the judgment of the court. In another, an action brought in July 1961 has not yet come to trail. The legal maxim" Justice delayed is Justice denied" is dramatically applicable in these cases.

Too often those who attempt to assert their Constitutional rights are intimidated. Prospective registrants are fired. Registration workers are arrested. In some instances, churches in which registration meetings are held have been burned. In one case where Negro tenant farmers chose to exercise their right to vote, it was necessary for the Justice Department to seek injunctions to halt their eviction and for the Department of Agriculture to help feed them from surplus stocks. Under these circumstances, continued delay in the granting of the franchise - particularly in counties where there is mass racial disfranchisement - permits the intent of the Congress to be openly flouted.

Federal executive action in such cases - no matter how speedy and how drastic - can never fully correct such abuses of power. It is necessary instead to free the forces of our democratic system within these areas by promptly insuring the franchise to all citizens, making it possible for their elected officials to be truly responsive to all their constituents.

The second and somewhat overlapping gap in these statutes is their failure to deal specifically with the most common forms of abuse of discretion on the part of local election officials who do not treat all applicants uniformly.

Objections were raised last year to the proposed literacy test bill, which attempted to speed up the enforcement of the right to vote by removing one important area of discretion from registration officials who used that discretion to exclude Negroes. Preventing that bill from coming to a vote did not make any less real the prevalence in many counties of the use of literacy and other voter qualification tests to discriminate against prospective Negro voters, contrary to the requirements of the 14th and 15th Amendments, and adding to the delays and difficulties encountered in securing the franchise for those denied it.

An indication of the magnitude of the overall problem, as well as the need for speedy action, is a recent five-state survey disclosing over 200 counties in which fewer than 15% of the Negroes of voting age are registered to vote. This cannot continue. I am, therefore, recommending legislation to deal with this problem of judicial delay and administrative abuse in four ways:

First, to provide for interim relief while voting suits are proceeding through the courts in areas of demonstrated need, temporary Federal voting referees should be appointed to determine the qualifications of applicants for registration and voting during the pendency of a lawsuit in any county in which fewer than 15% of the eligible number of persons of any race claimed to be discriminated against are registered to vote. Existing Federal law provides for the appointment of voting referees to receive and act upon applications for voting registration upon a court finding that a pattern or practice of discrimination exists. But to prevent a successful case from becoming an empty victory, insofar as the particular election is concerned, the proposed legislation would provide that, within these prescribed limits, temporary voting referees would be appointed to serve from the inception to the conclusion of the Federal voting suit, applying, however, only State law and State regulations. As officers of the court, their decisions would be subject to court scrutiny and review.

Second, voting suits brought under the Federal Civil Rights statutes should be accorded expedited treatment in the Federal courts, just as in many state courts election suits are given preference on the dockets on the sensible premise that, unless the right to vote can be exercised at a specific election, it is, to the extent of that election, lost forever.

Third, the law should specifically prohibit the application of different tests, standards, practices, or procedures for different applicants seeking to register and vote in federal election. Under present law, the courts can ultimately deal with the various forms of racial discrimination practiced by local registrars. But the task of litigation, and the time consumed in preparation and proof, should be lightened in every possible fashion. No one can rightfully contend that any voting registrar should be permitted to deny the vote to any qualified citizen, anywhere in this country, through discriminatory administration of qualifying tests, or upon the basis of minor errors in filling out a complicated form which seeks only information. Yet the Civil Rights Commission, and the cases brought by the Department of Justice, have compiled one discouraging example after another of obstacles placed in the path of Negroes seeking to register to vote at the same time that other applicants experience no difficulty whatsoever. Qualified Negroes, including those with college degrees, have been denied registration for their inability to give a "reasonable" interpretation of the Constitution. They have been required to complete their applications with unreasonable precision - or to secure registered voters to vouch for their identity - or to defer to white persons who want to register ahead of them - or they are otherwise subjected to exasperating delays. Yet uniformity of treatment is required by the dictates of both the Constitution and fair play - and this proposed statute, therefore, seeks to spell out that principle to ease the difficulties and delays of litigation. Limiting the proposal to voting qualifications in elections for Federal offices alone will clearly eliminate any Constitutional conflict.

Fourth, completion of the sixth grade should, with respect to Federal elections, constitute a presumption that the applicant is literate. Literacy tests pose especially difficult problems in determining voter qualification. The essentially subjective judgment involved in each individual case, and the difficulty of challenging that judgment, have made literacy tests one of the cruelest and most abused of all voter qualification tests. The incidence of such abuse can be eliminated, or at least drastically curtailed, by the proposed legislation providing that proof of completion of the sixth grade constitutes a presumption that the applicant is literate.

Finally, the 87th Congress - after 20 years of effort - passed and referred to the states for ratification a Constitutional Amendment to prohibit the levying of poll taxes as a condition to voting. Already thirteen states have ratified the proposed Amendment and in three more one body of the Legislature has acted. I urge every state legislature to take prompt action on this matter and to outlaw the poll tax - which has too long been an outmoded and arbitrary bar to voting participation by minority groups and others - as the 24th Amendment to the Constitution. This measure received bipartisan sponsorship and endorsement in the Congress - and I shall continue to work with governors and legislative leaders of both parties in securing adoption of the anti-poll tax amendment.

Nearly nine years have elapsed since the Supreme Court ruled that State laws requiring or permitting segregated schools violate the Constitution. That decision represented both good law and good judgment - it was both legally and morally right. Since that time it has become increasingly clear that neither violence nor legalistic evasions will be tolerated as a means of thwarting court-ordered desegregation, that closed schools are not an answer, and that responsible communities are able to handle the desegregation process in a calm and sensible manner. This is as it should be - for, as I stated to the Nation at the time of the Mississippi violence last September:

"Our Nation is founded on the principle that observance of the law is the eternal safeguard of liberty, and defiance of the law is the surest road to tyranny. The law which we obey includes the final rulings of the courts, as well as the enactments of our legislative bodies. Even among law abiding men, few laws are universally loved - but they are uniformly respected and not resisted.

"Americans are free to disagree with the law but not to disobey it. For in a government of laws and not of men, no man, however prominent or powerful, and no mob, however unruly or boisterous, is entitled to defy a court of law. If this country should ever reach the point where any man or group of men, by force or threat of force, could long defy the commands of our court and our Constitution, then no law would stand free from doubt, no judge would be sure of his writ, and no citizen would be safe from his neighbors."

The shameful violence which accompanied but did not prevent the end of segregation at the University of

Mississippi was an exception. State supported universities in Georgia and South Carolina met this test in recent years with calm and maturity, as did the state supported universities of Virginia, North Carolina, Florida, Texas, Louisiana, Tennessee, Arkansas and Kentucky in earlier years. In addition, progress toward the desegregation of education at all levels has made other notable and peaceful strides, including the following forward moves in the last two years alone:

Desegregation plans have been put into effect peacefully in the public schools of Atlanta, Dallas, New Orleans, Memphis and elsewhere, with over 60 school districts desegregated last year - frequently with the help of Federal persuasion and consultation, and in every case without incident or disorder.

Teacher training institutes financed under the National Defense Education Act are no longer held in colleges which refuse to accept students without regard to race, and this has resulted in a number of institutions opening their doors to Negro applicants voluntarily.

The same is now true of Institutes conducted by the National Science Foundation;

Beginning in September of this year, under the Aid to Impacted Area School Program, the Department of Health, Education, and Welfare will initiate a program of providing on-base facilities so that children living on military installations will no longer be required to attend segregated schools at Federal expense. These children should not be victimized by segregation merely because their fathers chose to serve in the armed forces and were assigned to an area where schools are operated on a segregated basis.

In addition, the Department of Justice and the Department of Health, Education, and Welfare have succeeded in obtaining voluntary desegregation in many other districts receiving "impacted area" school assistance; and, representing the Federal interest, have filed lawsuits to end segregation in a number of other districts.

The Department of Justice has also intervened to seek the opening of public schools in the case of Prince Edward County, Virginia, the only county in the Nation where there are no public schools, and where a bitter effort to thwart court decrees requiring desegregation has caused nearly 1500 out of 1800 school-age Negro children to go without any education for more than 3 years.

In these and other areas within its jurisdiction, the Executive Branch will continue its efforts to fulfill the Constitutional objective of an equal, non-segregated, educational opportunity for all children. Despite these efforts, however, progress toward primary and secondary school desegregation has still been too slow, often painfully so. Those children who are being denied their constitutional rights are suffering a loss which can never be regained, and which will leave scars which can never be fully healed. I have in the past expressed my belief that the full authority of the Fedewral government should be placed behind the achievement of school desegregation, in accordance with the command of the Constitution. One obvious area of Federal action is to help facilitate the transition to desegregation in those areas which are conforming or wish to conform their practices to the law.

Many of these communities lack the resources necessary
to eliminate segregation in their public schools while at
the same time assuring that educational standards will be
maintained and improved. The problem has been
compounded by the fact that the climate of mistrust in
many communities has left many school officials with no
qualified source to turn to for information and advice.

There is a need for technical assistance by the Office of
Education to assist local communities in preparing and
carrying out desegregation plans, including the supplying
of information on means which have been employed to
desegregate other schools successfully. There is also need
for financial assistance to enable those communities which
desire and need such assistance to employ specialized
personnel to cope with problems occasioned by
desegregation and to train school personnel to facilitate
the transition to desegregation. While some facilities for
providing this kind of assistance are presently available in
the Office of Education, they are not adequate to the task.

I recommend, therefore, a program of Federal technical
and financial assistance to aid school districts in the
process of desegregation in compliance with the
Constitution.

Finally, it is obvious that the unconstitutional and
outmoded concept of "separate but equal" does not belong
in the Federal statute books. This is particularly true with
respect to higher education, where peaceful desegregation
has been underway in practically every state for some
time. I repeat, therefore, this Administration's
recommendation of last year that this phrase be
eliminated from the Morrill Land Grant College Act.

The Commission on Civil Rights, established by the Civil Rights Act of 1957, has been in operation for more than five years and is scheduled to expire on November 30, 1963. During this time it has fulfilled its statutory mandate by investigating deprivations of the right to vote and denials of equal protection of the laws in education, employment, housing and the administration of justice. The Commission's reports and recommendations have provided the basis for remedial action both by Congress and the Executive Branch.

There are, of course, many areas Congress of denials of rights yet to be fully investigated. But the Commission is now in a position to provide even more useful service to the Nation. As more communities evidence a willingness to face frankly their problems of racial discrimination, there is an increasing need for expert guidance and assistance in devising workable programs for civil rights progress. Agencies of State and local government, industry, labor and community organizations, when faced with problems of segregation and racial tensions, all can benefit from information about how these problems have been solved in the past. The opportunity to seek an experienced and sympathetic forum on a voluntary basis can often open channels of communication between contending parties and help bring about the conditions necessary for orderly progress. And the use of public hearings - to contribute to public knowledge of the requirements of the Constitution and national policy - can create in these communities the atmosphere of understanding which is indispensable to peaceful and permanent solutions to racial problems.

The Federal Civil Rights Commission has the experience and capability to make a significant contribution toward achieving these objectives. It has advised the Executive branch not only about desirable policy changes but about the administrative techniques needed to make these changes effective. If, however, the Commission is to perform these additional services effectively, changes in its authorizing statute are necessary and it should be placed on a more stable and more permanent basis. A proposal that the Commission be made a permanent body would be a pessimistic prediction that our problems will never be solved. On the other hand, to let the experience and knowledge gathered by the Commission go to waste, by allowing it to expire, or by extending its life only for another two years with no change in responsibility, would ignore the very real contribution this agency can make toward meeting our racial problems. I recommend, therefore, that the Congress authorize the Civil Rights Commission to serve as a national civil rights clearing house providing information, advice, and technical assistance to any requesting agency, private or public; that in order to fulfill these new responsibilities, the Commission be authorized to concentrate its activities upon those problems within the scope of its statute which most need attention; and that the life of the Commission be extended for a term of at least four more years.

Racial discrimination in employment is especially injurious both to its victims and to the national economy. It results in a great waste of human resources and creates serious community problems. It is, moreover, inconsistent with the democratic principle that no man should be denied employment commensurate with his abilities because of his race or creed or ancestry.

The President's Committee on Equal Employment Opportunity, reconstituted by Executive Order in early

1961, has, under the leadership of the Vice President, taken significant steps to eliminate racial discrimination by those who do business with the Government. Hundreds of companies - covering 17 million jobs - have agreed to stringent nondiscriminatory provisions now standard in all Government contracts. One hundred four industrial concerns - including most of the Nation's major employers - have in addition signed agreements calling for an affirmative attack on discrimination in employment; and 117 labor unions, representing about 85% of the membership of the AFL-CIO, have signed similar agreements with the Committee. Comprehensive compliance machinery has been instituted to enforce these agreements. The Committee has received over 1,300 complaints in two years - more than in the entire 7-1/2 years of the Committee's prior existence - and has achieved corrective action on 72% of the cases handled - a heartening and unprecedented record. Significant results have been achieved in placing Negroes with contractors who previously employed whites only - and in the elevation of Negroes to a far higher proportion of professional, technical and supervisory jobs. Let me repeat my assurances that these provisions in Government contracts and the voluntary nondiscrimination agreements will be carefully monitored and strictly enforced.

In addition, the Federal Government, as an employer, has continued to pursue a policy of nondiscrimination in its employment and promotion programs. Negro high school and college graduates are now being intensively sought out and recruited. A policy of not distinguishing on grounds of race is not limited to the appointment of distinguished Negroes - although they have in fact been appointed to a record number of high policy-making judicial and administrative posts. There has also been a significant increase in the number of Negroes employed in the middle and upper grades of the career Federal service. In jobs paying $4,500 to $10,000 annually, for example, there was an increase of 20% in the number of Negroes during the year ending June 30, 1962 - over three times the rate of increase for all employees in those grades during the year. Career civil servants will continue to be employed and promoted on the basis of merit, and not color, in every agency of the Federal Government, including all regional and local offices.

This Government has also adopted a new Executive policy with respect to the organization of its employees. As part of this policy, only those Federal employee labor organizations that do not discriminate on grounds of race or color will be recognized.

Outside of Government employment, the National Labor Relations Board is now considering cases involving charges of racial discrimination against a number of union locals. I have directed the Department of Justice to participate in these cases and to urge the National Labor Relations Board to take appropriate action against racial discrimination in unions. It is my hope that administrative action and litigation will make unnecessary the enactment of legislation with respect to Union discrimination.

No act is more contrary to the spirit of our democracy and Constitution - or more rightfully resented by a Negro citizen who seeks only equal treatment - than the barring of that citizen from restaurants, hotels, theaters, recreational areas and other public accommodations and facilities.

Wherever possible, this Administration has dealt sternly with such acts. In 1961, the Justice Department and the Interstate Commerce Commission successfully took action to bring an end to discrimination in rail and bus facilities. In 1962, the fifteen airports still maintaining segregated facilities were persuaded to change their practices, thirteen voluntarily and two others after the Department of Justice brought legal action. As a result of these steps, systematic segregation in interstate transportation has virtually ceased to exist. No doubt isolated instances of discrimination in transportation terminals, restaurants, restrooms and other facilities will continue to crop up, but any such discrimination will be dealt with promptly.

In addition, restaurants and public facilities in buildings leased by the Federal Government have been opened up to all Federal employees in areas where previously they had been segregated. The General Services Administration no longer contracts for the lease of space in office buildings unless such facilities are available to all Federal employees without regard to race. This move has taken place without fanfare and practically without incident; and full equality of facilities will continue to be made available to all Federal employees in every state.

National parks, forests and other recreational areas - and the District of Columbia Stadium - are open to all without regard to race. Meetings sponsored by the Federal Government or addressed by Federal appointees are held in hotels and halls which do not practice discrimination or segregation. The Department of Justice has asked the Supreme Court to reverse the convictions of Negroes arrested for seeking to use public accommodations; and took action both through the Courts and the use of

Federal marshals to protect those who were testing the desegregation of transportation facilities.

In these and other ways, the Federal Government will continue to encourage and support action by state and local communities, and by private entrepreneurs, to assure all members of the public equal access to all public accommodations. A country with a "color blind" Constitution, and with no castes or classes among its citizens,cannot afford to do less.

The basic standard of nondiscrimination - which I earlier stated has now been applied by the Executive Branch to every area of its activity - affects other programs not listed above:

Although President Truman ordered the armed services of this country desegregated in 1948, it was necessary in 1962 to bar segregation formally and specifically in the Army and Air Force Reserves and in the training of all civil defense workers.

A new Executive Order on housing, as unanimously recommended by the Civil Rights Commission in 1959, prohibits discrimination in the sale, lease or use of housing owned or constructed in the future by the Federal Government or guaranteed under the FHA, VA and Farmers Home Administration program. With regard to existing property owned or financed through the Federal Government, the departments and agencies are directed to take every appropriate action to promote the termination of discriminatory practices that may exist. A President's Committee on Equal Housing Opportunity was created by the Order to implement its provisions.

A Committee on Equal Opportunity in the Armed Forces has been established to investigate and make recommendations regarding the treatment of minority groups, with special emphasis on off-base problems.

The U.S. Coast Guard Academy now has Negro students for the first time in its 87 years of existence.

The Department of Justice has increased its prosecution of police brutality cases, many of them in Northern states - and is assisting state and local police departments in meeting this problem.

State employee merit systems operating programs financed with Federal funds are now prohibited from discriminating on the basis of race or color.

The Justice Department is challenging the constitutionality of the "separate but equal" provisions which permit hospitals constructed with Federal funds to discriminate racially in the location of patients and the acceptance of doctors.

In short, the Executive Branch of the Federal Government, under this Administration, and in all of its activities, now stands squarely behind the principle of equal opportunity, without segregation or discrimination, in the employment of Federal funds, facilities and personnel. All officials at every level are charged with the responsibility of implementing this principle - and a formal interdepartmental action group, under White House chairmanship, oversees this effort and follows through on each directive. For the first time, the full force of Federal executive authority is being exerted in the battle against race discrimination.

The various steps which have been undertaken or which are proposed in this Message do not constitute a final answer to the problems of race discrimination in this country. They do not constitute a list of priorities - steps which can be taken by the Executive Branch and measures which can be taken by the Executive Branch and measures which can be enacted by the 88th Congress. Other measures directed toward these same goals will be favorably commented on and supported, as they have in the past - and they will be signed, if enacted into law.

In addition, it is my hope that this message will lend encouragement to those state and local governments - and to private organizations, corporations and individuals - who share my concern over the gap between our precepts and our practices. This is an effort in which every individual who asks what he can do for his country should be able and willing to take part. It is important,for example, for private citizens and local governments to support the State Department's effort to end the discriminatory treatment suffered by too many foreign diplomats, students and visitors of this country. But it is not enough to treat those from other lands with equality and dignity - the same treatment must be afforded to every American citizen.

The program outlined in this message should not provide the occasion for sectional bitterness. No state or section of this Nation can pretend a self-righteous role, for every area has its own civil rights problems.

Nor should the basic elements of this program be imperiled by partisanship. The proposals put forth are consistent with the platforms of both parties and with the positions of their leaders. Inevitably there will be disagreement about means and strategy. But I would hope that on issues of constitutional rights and freedom, as in matters affecting our national security, there is a fundamental unity among us that will survive partisan debate over particular issues.

The centennial of the issuance of the Emancipation Proclamation is an occasion for celebration, for a sober assessment of our failures, and for rededication to the goals of freedom. Surely there could be no more meaningful observance of the centennial than the enactment of effective civil rights legislation and the continuation of effective executive action.

Commencement Address
U.S. Air Force Academy
Colorado Springs, Colorado
June 5, 1963

I want to express my appreciation for becoming an instant graduate of this academy, and consider it a high honor.

Mr. Salinger, Press Secretary of the White House, received the following letter several days ago:

"*Dear Sir:*

"Would you desire to become an honorary member of the Air Force Cadet Wing for granting one small favor? Your name, Mr. Salinger, shall become more hallowed and revered than the combined memories of Generals Mitchell, Arnold, and Doolittle.

"My humble desire is that you convey a request from the Cadet Wing to the President. Sir, there are countless numbers of our group who are oppressed by Class 3 punishments, the bane of cadets everywhere. The President is our only hope for salvation. By granting amnesty to our oppressed brethren, he and you could end our anguish and depression.

"Please, sir, help us return to the ranks of the living so that we may work for the New Frontier with enthusiasm and vigor."

It is signed "Sincerely, Cadet Marvin B. Hopkins," who's obviously going to be a future General.

As Mr. Salinger wants to be honored with Generals Mitchell, Arnold, and Doolittle, I therefore take great pleasure in granting amnesty to all those who not only deserve it, but need it.

It is customary for speakers on these occasions to say in graduating addresses that commencement signifies the beginning instead of an end, yet this thought applies with particular force to those of you who are graduating from our Nation's service academies today, for today you receive not only your degrees, but also your commissions, and tomorrow you join with all those in the military service, in the foreign service, the civil service, and elsewhere - and one million of them serve outside our frontiers - who have chosen to serve the Great Republic at a turning point in our history. You will have an opportunity to help make that history - an opportunity for a service career more varied and demanding than any that has been opened to any officer corps in the history of any country.

There are some who might be skeptical of that assertion. They claim that the future of the Air Force is mortgaged to an obsolete weapons system, the manned aircraft, or that Air Force officers of the future will be nothing more than "silent silo sitters," but nothing could be further from the truth. It is this very onrush of technology which demands an expanding role for the Nation's Air Force and Air Force officers, and which guarantees that an Air Force career in the next 40 years will be even more changing and more challenging than the careers of the last 40 years.

For some of you will travel where no man has ever traveled before. Some of you will fly the fastest planes that have ever been built, reach the highest altitudes that man has ever gone to, and lift the heaviest payloads of any aviator in history. Some of you will hold in your hands the most awesome destructive power which any nation or any man has conceived. Some of you will work with the leaders of new nations which were not even nations a few years ago. Some of you will support guerrilla and counter-guerrilla operations that combine the newest techniques of warfare with the oldest techniques of the jungle, and some of you will help develop new planes that spread their wings in flight, detect other planes at an unheard-of distance, deliver new weapons with unprecedented accuracy, and survey the ground from incredible heights as a testament to our strong faith in the future of air power and the manned airplane.

I am announcing today that the United States will commit itself to an important new program in civilian aviation. Civilian aviation, long both the beneficiary and the benefactor of military aviation, is of necessity equally dynamic. Neither the economics nor the politics of international air competition permits us to stand still in this area. Today the challenging new frontier in commercial aviation and in military aviation is a frontier already crossed by the military - supersonic flight. Leading members of the administration under the chairmanship of the Vice President have been considering carefully the role to be played by the National Government in determining the economic and technical feasibility of an American commercial supersonic aircraft, and in the development of such an aircraft if it be feasible.

Having reviewed their recommendations, it is my judgment that this Government should immediately commence a new program in partnership with private industry to develop at the earliest practical date the prototype of a commercially successful supersonic transport superior to that being built in any other country of the world. An open, preliminary design competition will be initiated immediately among American airframe and powerplant manufacturers with a more detailed design phase to follow. If these initial phases do not produce an aircraft capable of transporting people and goods safely, swiftly, and at prices the traveler can afford and the airlines find profitable, we shall not go further.

But if we can build the best operational plane of this type - and I believe we can - then the Congress and the country should be prepared to invest the funds and effort necessary to maintain this Nation's lead in long-range aircraft, a lead we have held since the end of the Second World War, a lead we should make every responsible effort to maintain. Spurred by competition from across the Atlantic and by the productivity of our own companies, the Federal Government must pledge funds to supplement the risk capital to be contributed by private companies. It must then rely heavily on the flexibility and ingenuity of private enterprise to make the detailed decisions and to introduce successfully this new jet-age transport into worldwide service, and we are talking about a plane in the end of the 60's that will move ahead at a speed faster than Mach 2 to all corners of the globe. This commitment, I believe, is essential to a strong and forward-looking Nation, and indicates the future of the manned aircraft as we move into a missile age as well.

The fact that the greatest value of all of the weapons of massive retaliation lies in their ability to deter war does not diminish their importance, nor will national security in the years ahead be achieved simply by piling up bigger bombs or burying our missiles under bigger loads of concrete. For in an imperfect world where human folly has been the rule and not the exception, the surest way to bring on the war that can never happen is to sit back and assure ourselves it will not happen. The existence of mutual nuclear deterrents cannot be shrugged off as stalemate, for our national security in a period of rapid change will depend on constant reappraisal of our present doctrines, on alertness to new developments, on imagination and resourcefulness, and new ideas. Stalemate is a static term and not one of you would be here today if you believed you were entering an outmoded service requiring only custodial duties in a period of nuclear stalemate.

I am impressed by the extraordinary scholastic record, unmatched by any new college or university in this country, which has been made by the students and graduates of this Academy. Four Rhodes scholarships last year, two this year, and other selected scholarships, and also your record in the graduate record examination makes the people of this country proud of this Academy and the Air Force which made it possible.

This country is proud of the fact that more than one out of five of your all-military faculty has a doctor's degree, and all the rest have master's degrees. This is what we need for leadership in our military services, for the Air Force officer of today and tomorrow requires the broadest kind of scholarship to understand a most complex and changing world. He requires understanding and learning unmatched in the days before World War II. Any graduate of this Academy who serves in our Armed Forces will need to know economics and history, and international affairs, and languages. You will need an appreciation of other societies, and an understanding of our own Nation's purposes and policy.

General Norstad's leadership in NATO, General Smart's outstanding tour of duty as the senior military representative in Japan are examples of Air Force officers who use their broad talents for the benefit of our country. Many of you will have similar opportunities to represent this country in negotiations with our adversaries as well as our friends, working with international organizations, working in every way in the hundred free countries around the globe to help them maintain their freedom. Your major responsibilities, in the final analysis, will relate to military command. Some of your may be members of the Joint Chiefs of Staff and participate as advisers to the President who holds office.

Last October's crisis in the Caribbean amply demonstrated that military policy and power cannot and must not be separated from political and diplomatic decisions. Whatever the military motive and implications of the reckless attempt to put missiles on the island of Cuba, the political and psychological implications were equally important. We needed in October - and we had them and we shall need them in the future, and we shall have them - military commanders who are conscious of the enormous stakes in the nuclear age of every decision that they take, who are aware of the fact that there are no purely political decisions or purely military decisions; that every problem is a mixture of both, men who know the difference between vital interests and peripheral interests, who can maneuver military forces with judgment and precision, as well as courage and determination, and who can foresee the effects of military action on political policy. We need men, in short, who can cope with the challenges of a new political struggle, an armed doctrine which uses every weapon in the struggle around the globe.

We live in a world, in short, where the principal problems that we face are not susceptible to military solutions alone. The role of our military power, in essence, is, therefore, to free ourselves and our allies to pursue the goals of freedom without the danger of enemy attack, but we do not have a separate military policy, and a separate diplomatic policy, and a separate disarmament policy, and a separate foreign aid policy, all unrelated to each other. They are all bound up together in the policy of the United States. Our goal is a coherent, overall, national security policy, one that truly serves the best interests of this country and those who depend upon it. It is worth noting that all of the decisions which we now face today will come in increased numbers in the months and years ahead.

I want to congratulate all of you who have chosen the United States Air Force as a career. As far as any of us can now see in Washington in the days ahead, you will occupy positions of the highest responsibility, and merely because we move into a changing period of weapon technology, as well as political challenge - because, in fact, we move into that period - there is greater need for you than ever before. You, here today on this field, your colleagues at Omaha, Nebraska, or at Elgin in Florida, or who may be stationed in Western Europe, or men who are at sea in ships hundreds of miles from land, or soldiers in camps in Texas, or on the Island of Okinawa, they maintain the freedom by being on the ready. They maintain the freedom, the security, and the peace not only of the United States, but of the dozens of countries who are allied to us who are close to the Communist power, and who depend upon us and, in a sense, only upon us, for their freedom and security. These distant ships, these distant planes, these distant men keep the peace in a great half-circle stretching all the way from Berlin to South Korea. This is the role which history and our own determination has placed upon a country which lived most of its history in isolation and neutrality, and yet in the last 18 years has carried the burden for free people everywhere. I think that this is a burden which we accept willingly, recognizing that if this country does not accept it, no people will, recognizing that in the most difficult time in the whole life of freedom, the United States is called upon to play its greatest role. This is a role which we are proud to accept, and I am particularly proud to see the United States accept it in the presence of these young men who have committed themselves to the service of our country and to the cause of its freedom. I congratulate you all, and most of all, I congratulate your mothers and fathers who made it possible.

"Ich Bin Ein Berliner"
West Berlin, Germany
June 26, 1963

I am proud to come to this city as the guest of your distinguished Mayor, who has symbolized throughout the world the fighting spirit of West Berlin. And I am proud to visit the Federal Republic with your distinguished Chancellor who for so many years has committed Germany to democracy and freedom and progress, and to come here in the company of my fellow American, General Clay, who has been in this city during its great moments of crisis and will come again if ever needed.

Two thousand years ago the proudest boast was "*civis Romanus sum*." Today, in the world of freedom, the proudest boast is "*Ich bin ein Berliner*."

There are many people in the world who really don't understand, or say they don't, what is the great issue between the free world and the Communist world. Let them come to Berlin. There are some who say that communism is the wave of the future. Let them come to Berlin. And there are some who say in Europe and elsewhere we can work with the Communists. Let them come to Berlin. And there are even a few who say that it is true that communism is an evil system, but it permits us to make economic progress. *Lass' sie nach Berlin Kommen.* Let them come to Berlin.

Freedom has many difficulties and democracy is not perfect, but we have never had to put a wall up to keep our people in, to prevent them from leaving us. I want to say, on behalf of my countrymen, who live many miles away on the other side of the Atlantic, who are far distant from you, that they take the greatest pride that they have been able to share with you, even from a distance, the story of the last 18 years. I know of no town, no city, that has been besieged for 18 years that still lives with the vitality and the force, and the hope and the determination of the city of West Berlin. While the wall is the most obvious and vivid demonstration of the failures of the Communist system, for all the world to see, we take no satisfaction in it, for it is, as your Mayor has said, an offense not only against history but an offense against humanity, separating families, dividing husbands and wives and brothers and sisters, and dividing a people who wish to be joined together.

What is true of this city is true of Germany - real, lasting peace in Europe can never be assured as long as one German out of four is denied the elementary right of free men, and that is to make a free choice. In 18 years of peace and good faith, this generation of Germans has earned the right to be free, including the right to unite their families and their nation in lasting peace, with good will to all people. You live in a defended island of freedom, but your life is part of the main. So let me ask you, as I close, to lift your eyes beyond the dangers of today, to the hopes of tomorrow, beyond the freedom merely of this city of Berlin, or your country of Germany, to the advance of freedom everywhere, beyond the wall to the day of peace with justice, beyond yourselves and ourselves to all mankind.

Freedom is indivisible, and when one man is enslaved, all are not free. When all are free, then we can look forward to that day when this city will be joined as one and this country and this great Continent of Europe in a peaceful and hopeful globe. When that day finally comes, as it will, the people of West Berlin can take sober satisfaction in the fact that they were in the front lines for almost two decades.

All free men, wherever they may live, are citizens of Berlin, and, therefore, as a free man, I take pride in the words "*Ich bin ein Berliner.*"

Physical Fitness
Washington, DC
August 13, 1963

I have recently returned from a trip to Europe, where I saw many of the hundreds of thousands of young Americans who are in the front lines of the defense of freedom. These members of the American forces are trained in skills and weapons of a complexity and power hitherto unknown to fighting men. But despite all the advances of modern science and the sophisticated technology of modern warfare, it was clear to me that the capacity of our Army to withstand aggression will depend in the future, as always, on the hardihood and endurance, the physical fitness, of the American GI.

We have seen in World War II, in Korea and in the jungles of Southeast Asia that any weapon, no matter how brilliantly conceived, must depend for its effectiveness on the fighting trim of the soldier who uses it. And what is true for the weapons of war is also true for the instruments of peace. Whether it is the astronaut exploring the boundaries of space, or the overworked civil servant laboring into the night to keep a Government program going, the effectiveness and creativity of the individual must rest, in large measure, on his physical fitness and vitality.

The realization of this essential truth about human beings was a cornerstone of the first and perhaps the greatest civilization of the Western World - the society of ancient Greece. Happiness, as defined by the Greeks, is "the exercise of vital powers along lines of excellence in a life affording them scope." The Greeks knew it was necessary to have not only a free and inquiring mind, but a strong and active body to develop "glorious-limbed youth," as Pindar, the athlete's poet, wrote. The symbol of their dedication to physical hardihood was the Olympic Games. During these games, a truce of the gods was proclaimed so that all Greece might come to celebrate an event that had an almost mystical significance as a periodic renewal of the vital energies of the state. Kings and philosophers alike regarded triumph in the physical contests of Olympia as deserving the highest honors of the state, and themselves participated in the tests of skill and strength. No astronaut or statesman of today receives a more enthusiastic welcome from his fellow citizens than did the Olympic victors when they returned to their cities.

It was this society, with its almost religious veneration of physical fitness, that produced some of our most towering achievements of art, thought and political organization. Throughout history, we can trace the same theme. Whether it has been the triumphs of the vast empire of Rome, the flourishing of the arts in Renaissance Italy, or the literature of Elizabethan England, those societies that have produced great creative and political achievements have almost always given a high place to the physical vigor of the individual citizen. For it is only upon a foundation of individual hardiness and vitality that we can build an "exercise of vital powers along the lines of excellence."

We have found this true in our own country. Pioneers and patriots from our earliest days applied strength and vigor as well as intellect, courage and vision to the establishment of the nation and the protection of its freedom. President Theodore Roosevelt reminded us that "our country calls not for the life of ease, but for the life of strenuous endeavor." The recognition of this vital link between physical fitness and national greatness has caused great alarm over the declining strength and hardihood of our citizens.

In earlier days, it was much easier for an American to keep fit. Indeed, many of the conditions of daily life required him to do so. Today, much of that has changed. Where Abraham Lincoln had to walk miles to borrow a book, today a bookmobile would bring it to his door. Where a student once thought nothing of walking miles to school, today a school bus picks him up at the door. Instead of chopping firewood, we get regular delivery from the oil truck. Household gadgets of incredible variety have cut down or eliminated daily chores. Television and radio have made it possible to witness the most varied range of entertainment without ever moving from the easy chair.

No one would advocate a return to the drudgery or the limited range of available interests that preceded many of these modern conveniences. We value the increased scope for leisure and imagination that they have opened up. Nor can we hope to turn back the clock and restore the more primitive, although, at times, more satisfying, conditions of life in an earlier America. But we cannot let the very technology that is one of the fruits of our national vitality become an instrument of its decline and, consequently, of our greatness as a nation. For we face challenges in today's world of a difficulty and scope that require the fullest exercise of all our powers. And if we do not guard the precious heritage of our national vigor on which those powers depend, then there are strong and impatient people waiting to pick up the gauntlet that we can no longer bear.

Since we can no longer count upon the routine conditions of daily life to maintain our physical fitness, we have only one alternative to continued decline: that is the establishment of systematic and readily accessible fitness programs in every school and community in the nation. It was for this purpose that, two and a half years ago, I reorganized the President's Council on Youth Fitness under the leadership of one of the country's leading football coaches, Charles B. (Bud) Wilkinson of the University of Oklahoma.

This was the first systematic effort to establish programs designed to solve the problem of fitness. It came at a time when new investigations had proved that only 52 percent of Americans could pass the same fitness tests that were mastered by more than 90 percent of young Europeans, that 25 percent of our schoolchildren would fail a test that measured only the barest rudiments of fitness, and that many communities lacked programs adequate to meet the needs of our young people or to increase the physical vigor of our adults.

The first and continuing task of the Council was to focus national attention on physical fitness. Films were produced by private industry and distributed around the nation. The Advertising Council agreed to conduct a public-service campaign comparable to its efforts in behalf of War Bond sales and forest-fire prevention. Special materials were prepared for magazines, radio and television stations, newspapers and billboards. Booklets containing suggested programs for adult and school fitness, and for community recreation leaders were published. There was a nationwide conference, attended by representatives from 44 states, followed by the first of a series of Regional Fitness Clinics, designed to increase awareness of new techniques for physical development, which was conducted last October in California. More than 500 participants from thirty colleges and six states attended.

There were more dramatic, if unplanned events, ranging from a sudden flurry of 50-mile hikes to the scaling of a Japanese mountain by a Cabinet member. All of these have made the subject of American fitness a central topic of debate, discussion and concern throughout the nation. It has even entered into our folk humor. This increased national awareness is reflected in the White House mail, where fitness is one of the main subjects of correspondence by young and old alike.

Among the letters are those that merely describe personal activities, such as one from a Brooklyn schoolgirl, who reports: "I am happy about your Physical Fitness Plan. . . . I turn cartwheels every chance I get. My parents are going out of their minds because I am always on my hands instead of my feet." Or the 12-year-old boy from Pennsylvania, who writes: "I have took to mind what you have said about youth physical fitness. I not only take gym in school, but I set aside an hour each day to have my own gym." A young girl from Los Angeles proudly says: "Dear President Kennedy, I have walked 8 miles and I was thirsty."

Some of the letters ask questions or make requests. An Alabama schoolboy asks "Dear sir, would you please send me a sample of your physical fitness." One lad from Iowa wanted us to write him an excuse from the regular physical-education program so that he can follow his own schedule of preparing for the football season, and added the caution: "Please do not say on TV or radio."

Humorous or serious, these letters and thousands more reflect the immense growth in national concern since the Council started its work.

We have never viewed the Council as a national department of physical education. It is not to become a large department, and its staff has been limited to four full-time employees with limited administrative funds. Rather, it is a catalyst to provide information and stimulus to the wide range of school systems, private groups, local communities and individual households that alone possess the intimacy of contact essential to make physical fitness an accepted goal and part of daily life.

In this effort, there has been much progress. Thirty-two states now have State Fitness Councils, and last year alone, 13 strengthened their physical-education requirements. Twenty-one now offer special summer programs, more than half of which have been started since 1960.

This increased interest by the states has been reflected in school activities. The number of schools conducting fitness programs has increased 20 percent since the 1961-62 school year, and today, in nine states, every elementary schoolchild has a daily physical-education program. In 1960, fewer than half of the nation's secondary schools tested their students for physical fitness. This year, 96 percent conducted such tests.

Not all of the forward strides can be measured by these statistics. Private groups ranging from 4-H Clubs to the YMCA have developed programs in cooperation with the Council, and the American Medical Association has emphasized the urgent need for physical-fitness programs and periodic health checkups in the elementary schools.

Increased emphasis and expanded programs are already being reflected in improved performance. When it began its work, the Council undertook a series of pilot studies in schools in seven states. The first results showed that only 53 percent of the students examined could pass a minimum-achievement test; this year, 79 percent passed the same tests. The number passing a more comprehensive test in the same period rose from 10 percent to 21 percent. Many universities also report a steady rise in the physical ability of their students. The number passing the Yale Physical Fitness test rose from 34 percent in 1960 to 43 percent in 1961; at Springfield College in the same period, the Physical Fitness Index rose from subnormal to above normal.

These figures can be supplemented with hundreds of stories of individual achievement and progress, such as that of the nine-year-old Missouri schoolboy whose legs were seriously affected by polio at the age of one. To him, regular exercise in a fitness program has meant entering upon a new life. He is now the pull-up champion of his class, bat boy for the local baseball team - and a well-above-average student.

The advances are encouraging, but we still have far to go. Twenty percent of all the country's schools have no regular fitness program, and 20 percent of our schoolchildren cannot pass a minimum test. Eighty percent cannot pass all the parts of a more comprehensive examination. We are still far from our goal of a daily, effective program for every schoolchild. And we have barely begun to work on the vast problem of adult fitness.

I recently had a letter from a student in a U.S. Army school in Munich, Germany. He wrote: "The purpose of my writing is to congratulate you on your physical-fitness program. All the students in my class take part in the program with great interest. Through the program, we are developing an interest in fair play with each other. The responsibility through our training gives us great pride and an understanding of our responsibility as Americans."

If our future is eventually to be entrusted to youngsters like this, then we need have little cause for concern about America. The fitness of our people is one of the foundation stones of our national greatness. It will help determine our capacity to respond to the many challenges of this time of change and conflict. But it has an even deeper significance. For fitness is not something that can be imposed by a government or by laws. It will not be produced by coercion or exhortation from above. It depends upon the will and the energy of those thousands of local and private groups that make up the fabric of our society. And it depends, preeminently, on the individual.

I hope that all parents who share my concern will inquire about the physical-fitness programs in their schools. I hope that every active American - particularly if he is a young American - will take part in such a program, for his own good and for his country's good.

Address to the General Assembly of the United Nations
New York, NY
September 20, 1963

We meet again in the quest for peace.

Twenty-four months ago, when I last had the honor of addressing this body, the shadow of fear lay darkly across the world. The freedom of West Berlin was in immediate peril. Agreement on a neutral Laos seemed remote. The mandate of the United Nations in the Congo was under fire. The financial outlook for this organization was in doubt. Dag Hammarskjold was dead. The doctrine of troika was being pressed in his place, and atmospheric nuclear tests had been resumed by the Soviet Union.

Those were anxious days for mankind - and some men wondered aloud whether this organization could survive. But the 16th and 17th General Assemblies achieved not only survival but progress. Rising to its responsibility, the United Nations helped reduce the tensions and helped to hold back the darkness.

Today the clouds have lifted a little so that new rays of hope can break through. The pressures on West Berlin appear to be temporarily eased. Political unity in the Congo has been largely restored. A neutral coalition in Laos, while still in difficulty, is at least in being. The integrity of the United Nations Secretariat has been reaffirmed. A United Nations Decade of Development is under way. And, for the first time in 17 years of effort, a specific step has been taken to limit the nuclear arms race.

I refer, of course, to the treaty to ban nuclear tests in the atmosphere, outer space, and under water - concluded by the Soviet Union, the United Kingdom, and the United States - and already signed by nearly 100 countries. It has been hailed by people the world over who are thankful to be free from the fears of nuclear fallout, and I am confident that on next Tuesday at 10:30 in the morning it will receive the overwhelming endorsement of the Senate of the United States.

The world has not escaped from the darkness. The long shadows of conflict and crisis envelop us still. But we meet today in an atmosphere of rising hope, and at a moment of comparative calm. My presence here today is not a sign of crisis, but of confidence. I am not here to report on a new threat to the peace or new signs of war. I have come to salute the United Nations and to show the support of the American people for your daily deliberations.

For the value of this body's work is not dependent on the existence of emergencies - nor can the winning of peace consist only of dramatic victories. Peace is a daily, a weekly, a monthly process, gradually changing opinions, slowly eroding old barriers, quietly building new structures. And however undramatic the pursuit of peace, that pursuit must go on.

Today we may have reached a pause in the cold war - but that is not a lasting peace. A test ban treaty is a milestone - but it is not the millennium. We have not been released from our obligations - we have been given an opportunity. And if we fail to make the most of this moment and this momentum - if we convert our new-found hopes and understandings into new walls and weapons of hostility -

if this pause in the cold war merely leads to its renewal and not to its end - then the indictment of posterity will rightly point its finger at us all. But if we can stretch this pause into a period of cooperation - if both sides can now gain new confidence and experience in concrete collaborations for peace - if we can now be as bold and farsighted in the control of deadly weapons as we have been in their creation - then surely this first small step can be the start of a long and fruitful journey.

The task of building the peace lies with the leaders of every nation, large and small. For the great powers have no monopoly on conflict or ambition. The cold war is not the only expression of tension in this world - and the nuclear race is not the only arms race. Even little wars are dangerous in a nuclear world. The long labor of peace is an undertaking for every nation - and in this effort none of us can remain unaligned. To this goal none can be uncommitted.

The reduction of global tension must not be an excuse for the narrow pursuit of self-interest. If the Soviet Union and the United States, with all of their global interests and closing commitments of ideology, and with nuclear weapons still aimed at each other today, can find areas of common interest and agreement, then surely other nations can do the same - nations caught in regional conflicts, in racial issues, or in the death throes of old colonialism. Chronic disputes which divert precious resources from the needs of the people or drain the energies of both sides serve the interests of no one - and the badge of responsibility in the modern world is a willingness to seek peaceful solutions.

It is never too early to try; and it's never too late to talk; and it's high time that many disputes on the agenda of this Assembly were taken off the debating schedule and placed on the negotiating table.

The fact remains that the United States, as a major nuclear power, does have a special responsibility in the world. It is, in fact, a threefold responsibility - a responsibility to our own citizens; a responsibility to the people of the whole world who are affected by our decisions; and to the next generation of humanity. We believe the Soviet Union also has these special responsibilities - and that those responsibilities require our two nations to concentrate less on our differences and more on the means of resolving them peacefully. For too long both of us have increased our military budgets, our nuclear stockpiles, and our capacity to destroy all life on this hemisphere - human, animal, vegetable - without any corresponding increase in our security.

Our conflicts, to be sure, are real. Our concepts of the world are different. No service is performed by failing to make clear our disagreements. A central difference is the belief of the American people in self-determination for all people.

We believe that the people of Germany and Berlin must be free to reunite their capital and their country.

We believe that the people of Cuba must be free to secure the fruits of the revolution that have been betrayed from within and exploited from without.

In short, we believe that all the world - in Eastern Europe as well as Western, in Southern Africa as well as

Northern, in old nations as well as new - that people must be free to choose their own future, without discrimination or dictation, without coercion or subversion.

These are the basic differences between the Soviet Union and the United States, and they cannot be concealed. So long as they exist, they set limits to agreement, and they forbid the relaxation of our vigilance. Our defense around the world will be maintained for the protection of freedom - and our determination to safeguard that freedom will measure up to any threat or challenge.

But I would say to the leaders of the Soviet Union, and to their people, that if either of our countries is to be fully secure, we need a much better weapon than the H-bomb - a weapon better than ballistic missiles or nuclear submarines - and that better weapon is peaceful cooperation.

We have, in recent years, agreed on a limited test ban treaty, on an emergency communications link between our capitals, on a statement of principles for disarmament, on an increase in cultural exchange, on cooperation in outer space, on the peaceful exploration of the Antarctic, and on tempering last year's crisis over Cuba.

I believe, therefore, that the Soviet Union and the United States, together with their allies, can achieve further agreements - agreements which spring from our mutual interest in avoiding mutual destruction.

There can be no doubt about the agenda of further steps. We must continue to seek agreements on measures which prevent war by accident or miscalculation. We must continue to seek agreement on safeguards against surprise attack, including observation posts at key points. We must continue to seek agreement on further measures to curb the nuclear arms race, by controlling the transfer of nuclear weapons, converting fissionable materials to peaceful purposes, and banning underground testing, with adequate inspection and enforcement. We must continue to seek agreement on a freer flow of information and people from East to West and West to East.

We must continue to seek agreement, encouraged by yesterday's affirmative response to this proposal by the Soviet Foreign Minister, on an arrangement to keep weapons of mass destruction out of outer space. Let us get our negotiators back to the negotiating table to work out a practicable arrangement to this end.

In these and other ways, let us move up the steep and difficult path toward comprehensive disarmament, securing mutual confidence through mutual verification, and building the institutions of peace as we dismantle the engines of war. We must not let failure to agree on all points delay agreements where agreement is possible. And we must not put forward proposals for propaganda purposes.

Finally, in a field where the United States and the Soviet Union have a special capacity - in the field of space - there is room for new cooperation, for further joint efforts in the regulation and exploration of space. I include among these possibilities a joint expedition to the moon. Space offers no problems of sovereignty; by resolution of this Assembly, the members of the United Nations have foresworn any claim to territorial rights in outer space or on celestial bodies, and declared that international law and the United Nations Charter will apply. Why, therefore, should man's first flight to the moon be a matter of national competition? Why should the United States and the Soviet Union, in preparing for such expeditions, become involved in immense duplications of research, construction, and expenditure? Surely we should explore whether the scientists and astronauts of our two countries - indeed of all the world - cannot work together in the conquest of space, sending some day in this decade to the moon not the representatives of a single nation, but the representatives of all of our countries.

All these and other new steps toward peaceful cooperation may be possible. Most of them will require on our part full consultation with our allies - for their interests are as much involved as our own, and we will not make an agreement at their expense. Most of them will require long and careful negotiation. And most of them will require a new approach to the cold war - a desire not to "bury" one's adversary, but to compete in a host of peaceful arenas, in ideas, in production, and ultimately in service to all mankind.

The contest will continue - the contest between those who see a monolithic world and those who believe in diversity - but it should be a contest in leadership and responsibility instead of destruction, a contest in achievement instead of intimidation. Speaking for the United States of America, I welcome such a contest. For we believe that truth is stronger than error - and that freedom is more enduring than coercion. And in the contest for a better life, all the world can be a winner.

The effort to improve the conditions of man, however, is not a task for the few. It is the task of all nations - acting alone, acting in groups, acting in the United Nations, for plague and pestilence, and plunder and pollution, the hazards of nature, and the hunger of children are the foes of every nation. The earth, the sea, and the air are the concern of every nation. And science, technology, and education can be the ally of every nation.

Never before has man had such capacity to control his own environment, to end thirst and hunger, to conquer poverty and disease, to banish illiteracy and massive human misery. We have the power to make this the best generation of mankind in the history of the world - or to make it the last.

The United States since the close of the war has sent over $100 billion worth of assistance to nations seeking economic viability. And 2 years ago this week we formed a Peace Corps to help interested nations meet the demand for trained manpower. Other industrialized nations whose economies were rebuilt not so long ago with some help from us are now in turn recognizing their responsibility to the less developed nations.

The provision of development assistance by individual nations must go on. But the United Nations also must play a larger role in helping bring to all men the fruits of modern science and industry. A United Nations conference on this subject held earlier this year at Geneva opened new vistas for the developing countries. Next year a United Nations Conference on Trade will consider the needs of these nations for new markets. And more than four-fifths of the entire United Nations system can be found today mobilizing the weapons of science and technology for the United Nations' Decade of Development.

But more can be done.

A world center for health communications under the World Health Organization could warn of epidemics and the adverse effects of certain drugs as well as transmit the results of new experiments and new discoveries.

Regional research centers could advance our common medical knowledge and train new scientists and doctors for new nations.

A global system of satellites could provide communication and weather information for all corners of the earth.

A worldwide program of conservation could protect the forest and wild game preserves now in danger of extinction for all time, improve the marine harvest of food from our oceans, and prevent the contamination of air and water by industrial as well as nuclear pollution.

And, finally, a worldwide program of farm productivity and food distribution, similar to our country's "Food for Peace" program, could now give every child the food he needs.

But man does not live by bread alone - and the members of this organization are committed by the Charter to promote and respect human rights. Those rights are not respected when a Buddhist priest is driven from his pagoda, when a synagogue is shut down, when a Protestant church cannot open a mission, when a Cardinal is forced into hiding, or when a crowded church service is bombed.

The United States of America is opposed to discrimination and persecution on grounds of race and religion anywhere in the world, including our own Nation. We are working to right the wrongs of our own country.

Through legislation and administrative action, through moral and legal commitment, this Government has launched a determined effort to rid our Nation of discrimination which has existed far too long - in education, in housing, in transportation, in employment, in the civil service, in recreation, and in places of public accommodation. And therefore, in this or any other forum, we do not hesitate to condemn racial or religious injustice, whether committed or permitted by friend or foe.

I know that some of you have experienced discrimination in this country. But I ask you to believe me when I tell you that this is not the wish of most Americans - that we share your regret and resentment - and that we intend to end such practices for all time to come, not only for our visitors, but for our own citizens as well.

I hope that not only our Nation but all other multiracial societies will meet these standards of fairness and justice. We are opposed to apartheid and all forms of human oppression. We do not advocate the rights of black Africans in order to drive out white Africans. Our concern is the right of all men to equal protection under the law - and since human rights are indivisible, this body cannot stand aside when those rights are abused and neglected by any member state.

New efforts are needed if this Assembly's Declaration of Human Rights, now 15 years old, is to have full meaning.

And new means should be found for promoting the free expression and trade of ideas - through travel and communication, and through increased exchanges of people, and books, and broadcasts. For as the world renounces the competition of weapons, competition in ideas must flourish - and that competition must be as full and as fair as possible.

The United States delegation will be prepared to suggest to the United Nations initiatives in the pursuit of all the goals. For this is an organization for peace - and peace cannot come without work and without progress.

The peacekeeping record of the United Nations has been a proud one, though its tasks are always formidable. We are fortunate to have the skills of our distinguished Secretary General and the brave efforts of those who have been serving the cause of peace in the Congo, in the Middle East, in Korea and Kashmir, in West New Guinea and Malaysia. But what the United Nations has done in the past is less important than the tasks for the future. We cannot take its peacekeeping machinery for granted. That machinery must be soundly financed - which it cannot be if some members are allowed to prevent it from meeting its obligations by failing to meet their own. The United Nations must be supported by all those who exercise their franchise here. And its operations must be backed to the end.

Too often a project is undertaken in the excitement of a crisis and then it begins to lose its appeal as the problems drag on and the bills pile up. But we must have the steadfastness to see every enterprise through.

It is, for example, most important not to jeopardize the extraordinary United Nations gains in the Congo. The nation which sought this organization's help only 3 years ago has now asked the United Nations' presence to remain a little longer. I believe this Assembly should do what is necessary to preserve the gains already made and to protect the new nation in its struggle for progress. Let us complete what we have started. For "no man who puts his hand to the plow and looks back," as the Scriptures tell us, "no man who puts his hand to the plow and looks back is fit for the Kingdom of God."

I also hope that the recent initiative of several members in preparing standby peace forces for United Nations call will encourage similar commitments by others. This Nation remains ready to provide logistic and other material support. Policing, moreover, is not enough without provision for pacific settlement. We should increase the resort to special missions of fact-finding and conciliation, make greater use of the International Court of Justice, and accelerate the work of the International Law Commission.

The United Nations cannot survive as a static organization. Its obligations are increasing as well as its size. Its Charter must be changed as well as its customs. The authors of that Charter did not intend that it be frozen in perpetuity. The science of weapons and war has made us all, far more than 18 years ago in San Francisco, one world and one human race, with one common destiny. In such a world, absolute sovereignty no longer assures us of absolute security. The conventions of peace must pull abreast and then ahead of the inventions of war. The United Nations, building on its successes and learning from its failures, must be developed into a genuine world security system.

But peace does not rest in charters and covenants alone. It lies in the hearts and minds of all people. And if it is cast out there, then no act, no pact, no treaty, no organization can hope to preserve it without the support and the wholehearted commitment of all people. So let us not rest all our hopes on parchment and on paper; let us strive to build peace, a desire for peace, a willingness to work for peace, in the hearts and minds of all of our people. I believe that we can. I believe the problems of human destiny are not beyond the reach of human beings.

Two years ago I told this body that the United States had proposed, and was willing to sign, a limited test ban treaty. Today that treaty has been signed. It will not put an end to war. It will not remove basic conflicts. It will not secure freedom for all. But it can be a lever, and Archimedes, in explaining the principles of the lever, was said to have declared to his friends: "Give me a place where I can stand - and I shall move the world."

My fellow inhabitants of this planet: Let us take our stand here in this Assembly of nations. And let us see if we, in our own time, can move the world to a just and lasting peace.

The Ungiven Speech
Dallas, TX
November 22, 1963

I am honored to have this invitation to address the annual meeting of the Dallas Citizens Council, joined by the members of the Dallas Assembly - and pleased to have this opportunity to salute the Graduate Research Center of the Southwest.

It is fitting that these two symbols of Dallas progress are united in the sponsorship of this meeting. For they represent the best qualities, I am told, of leadership and learning in this city - and leadership and learning are indispensable to each other. The advancement of learning depends on community leadership for financial and political support, and the products of that learning, in turn, are essential to the leadership's hopes for continued progress and prosperity. It is not a coincidence that those communities possessing the best in research and graduate facilities - from MIT to Cal Tech - tend to attract the new and growing industries. I congratulate those of you here in Dallas who have recognized these basic facts through the creation of the unique and forward-looking Graduate Research Center.

This link between leadership and learning is not only essential at the community level. It is even more indispensable in world affairs. Ignorance and misinformation can handicap the progress of a city or a company, but they can, if allowed to prevail in foreign policy, handicap this country's security. In a world of complex and continuing problems, in a world full of frustrations and irritations, America's leadership must be guided by the lights of learning and reason - or else those who confuse rhetoric with reality and the plausible with the possible will gain the popular ascendancy with their seemingly swift and simple solutions to every world problem.

There will always be dissident voices heard in the land, expressing opposition without alternatives, finding fault but never favor, perceiving gloom on every side and seeking influence without responsibility. Those voices are inevitable.

But today other voices are heard in the land - voices preaching doctrines wholly unrelated to reality, wholly unsuited to the sixties, doctrines which apparently assume that words will suffice without weapons, that vituperation is as good as victory and that peace is a sign of weakness. At a time when the national debt is steadily being reduced in terms of its burden on our economy, they see that debt as the greatest single threat to our security. At a time when we are steadily reducing the number of Federal employees serving every thousand citizens, they fear those supposed hordes of civil servants far more than the actual hordes of opposing armies.

We cannot expect that everyone, to use the phrase of a decade ago, will "talk sense to the American people." But we can hope that fewer people will listen to nonsense. And the notion that this Nation is headed for defeat through deficit, or that strength is but a matter of slogans, is nothing but just plain nonsense.

I want to discuss with you today the status of our strength and our security because this question clearly calls for the most responsible qualities of leadership and the most enlightened products of scholarship. For this Nation's strength and security are not easily or cheaply obtained, nor are they quickly and simply explained. There are many kinds of strength and no one kind will suffice. Overwhelming nuclear strength cannot stop a guerrilla war. Formal pacts of alliance cannot stop internal subversion. Displays of material wealth cannot stop the disillusionment of diplomats subjected to discrimination.

Above all, words alone are not enough. The United States is a peaceful nation. And where our strength and determination are clear, our words need merely to convey conviction, not belligerence. If we are strong, our strength will speak for itself. If we are weak, words will be of no help.

I realize that this Nation often tends to identify turning-points in world affairs with the major addresses which preceded them. But it was not the Monroe Doctrine that kept all Europe away from this hemisphere - it was the strength of the British fleet and the width of the Atlantic Ocean. It was not General Marshall's speech at Harvard which kept communism out of Western Europe - it was the strength and stability made possible by our military and economic assistance.

In this administration also it has been necessary at times to issue specific warnings - warnings that we could not stand by and watch the Communists conquer Laos by force, or intervene in the Congo, or swallow West Berlin, or maintain offensive missiles on Cuba. But while our goals were at least temporarily obtained in these and other instances, our successful defense of freedom was due not to the words we used, but to the strength we stood ready to use on behalf of the principles we stand ready to defend.

This strength is composed of many different elements, ranging from the most massive deterrents to the most subtle influences. And all types of strength are needed - no one kind could do the job alone. Let us take a moment, therefore, to review this Nation's progress in each major area of strength.

First, as Secretary McNamara made clear in his address last Monday, the strategic nuclear power of the United States has been so greatly modernized and expanded in the last 1,000 days, by the rapid production and deployment of the most modern missile systems, that any and all potential aggressors are clearly confronted now with the impossibility of strategic victory - and the certainty of total destruction - if by reckless attack they should ever force upon us the necessity of a strategic reply.

In less than 3 years, we have increased by 50 percent the number of Polaris submarines scheduled to be in force by the next fiscal year, increased by more than 70 percent our total Polaris purchase program, increased by more than 75 percent our Minuteman purchase program, increased by 50 percent the portion of our strategic bombers on 15-minute alert, and increased by 100 percent the total number of nuclear weapons available in our strategic alert forces. Our security is further enhanced by the steps we have taken regarding these weapons to improve the speed and certainty of their response, their readiness at all times to respond, their ability to survive an attack, and their ability to be carefully controlled and directed through secure command operations.

But the lessons of the last decade have taught us that freedom cannot be defended by strategic nuclear power alone. We have, therefore, in the last 3 years accelerated the development and deployment of tactical nuclear weapons, and increased by 60 percent the tactical nuclear forces deployed in Western Europe.

Nor can Europe or any other continent rely on nuclear forces alone, whether they are strategic or tactical. We have radically improved the readiness of our conventional forces - increased by 45 percent the number of combat-ready Army divisions, increased by 100 percent the procurement of modern Army weapons and equipment, increased by 100 percent our ship construction, conversion, and modernization program, increased by 100 percent our procurement of tactical aircraft, increased by 30 percent the number of tactical air squadrons, and increased the strength of the Marines. As last month's "Operation Big Lift" - which originated here in Texas - showed so clearly, this Nation is prepared as never before to move substantial numbers of men in surprisingly little time to advanced positions anywhere in the world. We have increased by 175 percent the procurement of airlift aircraft, and we have already achieved a 75 percent increase in our existing strategic airlift capability. Finally, moving beyond the traditional roles of our military forces, we have achieved an increase of nearly 600 percent in our special forces - those forces that are prepared to work with our allies and friends against the guerrillas, saboteurs, insurgents and assassins who threaten freedom in a less direct but equally dangerous manner.

But American military might should not and need not stand alone against the ambitions of international communism. Our security and strength, in the last analysis, directly depend on the security and strength of others, and that is why our military and economic assistance plays such a key role in enabling those who live on the periphery of the Communist world to maintain their independence of choice. Our assistance to these nations can be painful, risky and costly, as is true in Southeast Asia today. But we dare not weary of the task. For our assistance makes possible the stationing of 3-5 million allied troops along the Communist frontier at one-tenth the cost of maintaining a comparable number of American soldiers. A successful Communist breakthrough in these areas, necessitating direct United States intervention, would cost us several times as much as our entire foreign aid program, and might cost us heavily in American lives as well.

About 70 percent of our military assistance goes to nine key countries located on or near the borders of the Communist bloc - nine countries confronted directly or indirectly with the threat of Communist aggression - Viet Nam, Free China, Korea, India, Pakistan, Thailand, Greece, Turkey, and Iran. No one of these countries possesses on its own the resources to maintain the forces which our own Chiefs of Staff think needed in the common interest. Reducing our efforts to train, equip, and assist their armies can only encourage Communist penetration and require in time the increased overseas deployment of American combat forces. And reducing the economic help needed to bolster these nations that undertake to help defend freedom can have the same disastrous result. In short, the $50 billion we spend each year on our own defense could well be ineffective without the $4 billion required for military and economic assistance.

Our foreign aid program is not growing in size; it is, on the contrary, smaller now than in previous years. It has had its weaknesses, but we have undertaken to correct them. And the proper way of treating weaknesses is to replace them with strength, not to increase those weaknesses by emasculating essential programs. Dollar for dollar, in or out of government, there is no better form of investment in our national security than our much-abused foreign aid program. We cannot afford to lose it. We can afford to maintain it. We can surely afford, for example, to do as much for our 19 needy neighbors of Latin America as the Communist bloc is sending to the island of Cuba alone.

I have spoken of strength largely in terms of the deterrence and resistance of aggression and attack. But, in today's world, freedom can be lost without a shot being fired, by ballots as well as bullets. The success of our leadership is dependent upon respect for our mission in the world as well as our missiles - on a clearer recognition of the virtues of freedom as well as the evils of tyranny.

That is why our Information Agency has doubled the shortwave broadcasting power of the Voice of America and increased the number of broadcasting hours by 30 percent, increased Spanish language broadcasting to Cuba and Latin America from 1 to 9 hours a day, increased seven-fold to more than 3.5 million copies the number of American books being translated and published for Latin American readers, and taken a host of other steps to carry our message of truth and freedom to all the far corners of the earth.

And that is also why we have regained the initiative in the exploration of outer space, making an annual effort greater than the combined total of all space activities undertaken during the fifties, launching more than 130 vehicles into earth orbit, putting into actual operation valuable weather and communications satellites, and making it clear to all that the United States of America has no intention of finishing second in space.

This effort is expensive - but it pays its own way, for freedom and for America. For there is no longer any fear in the free world that a Communist lead in space will become a permanent assertion of supremacy and the basis of military superiority. There is no longer any doubt about the strength and skill of American science, American industry, American education, and the American free enterprise system. In short, our national space effort represents a great gain in, and a great resource of, our national strength - and both Texas and Texans are contributing greatly to this strength.

Finally, it should be clear by now that a nation can be no stronger abroad than she is at home. Only an America which practices what it preaches about equal rights and social justice will be respected by those whose choice affects our future. Only an America which has fully educated its citizens is fully capable of tackling the complex problems and perceiving the hidden dangers of the world in which we live. And only an America which is growing and prospering economically can sustain the worldwide defenses of freedom, while demonstrating to all concerned the opportunities of our system and society.

It is clear, therefore, that we are strengthening our security as well as our economy by our recent record increases in national income and output - by surging ahead of most of Western Europe in the rate of business expansion and the margin of corporate profits, by maintaining a more stable level of prices than almost any of our overseas competitors, and by cutting personal and corporate income taxes by some $11 billion, as I have proposed, to assure this Nation of the longest and strongest expansion in our peacetime economic history.

This Nation's total output - which 3 years ago was at the $500 billion mark - will soon pass $600 billion, for a record rise of over $100 billion in 3 years. For the first time in history we have 70 million men and women at work. For the first time in history average factory earnings have exceeded $100 a week. For the first time in history corporation profits after taxes - which have risen 43 percent in less than 3 years - have an annual level of $27.4 billion.

My friends and fellow citizens: I cite these facts and figures to make it clear that America today is stronger than ever before. Our adversaries have not abandoned their ambitions, our dangers have not diminished, our vigilance cannot be relaxed. But now we have the military, the scientific, and the economic strength to do whatever must be done for the preservation and promotion of freedom.

That strength will never be used in pursuit of aggressive ambitions - it will always be used in pursuit of peace. It will never be used to promote provocations - it will always be used to promote the peaceful settlement of disputes.

We in this country, in this generation, are - by destiny rather than choice - the watchmen on the walls of world freedom. We ask, therefore, that we may be worthy of our power and responsibility, that we may exercise our strength with wisdom and restraint, and that we may achieve in our time and for all time the ancient vision of "peace on earth, good will toward men." That must always be our goal, and the righteousness of our cause must always underlie our strength. For as was written long ago, "except the Lord keep the city, the watchman waketh but in vain."

BIBLIOGRAPHY

Anson, Robert Sam. *"They've Killed the President!": The Search for the Murderers of John F. Kennedy.* New York, NY: Bantam Books, 1975.

Bernstein, Irving. *Promises Kept: John F. Kennedy's New Frontier.* New York, NY: Oxford University Press, 1991.

Beschloss, Michael R. *The Crisis Years: Kennedy and Krushchev, 1960-1963.* New York, NY: Edward Burlingame Books, 1991.

Bishop, Jim. *The Day Kennedy Was Shot.* New York, NY: Funk & Wagnalls, 1968.

Bradlee, Benjamin. *Conversations with Kennedy.* New York, NY: Norton, 1975.

Brauer, Carl M. *John F. Kennedy and the Second Reconstruction.* New York, NY: Columbia University Press, 1977.

Burns, James MacGregor. *John F. Kennedy: A Profile.* New York, NY: Harcourt, Brace & World, 1961.

Carr, William H.A. *JFK, The Life and Death of a President.* New York, NY: Lancer Books, 1964.

Chomsky, Noam. *Rethinking Camelot: JFK, the Vietnam War, and U.S. Political Culture.* Boston: South End Press, 1993.

Crown, James Tracy, and George P. Penty. *Kennedy in Power.* New York, NY: Ballantine Books, 1961.

Donald, Aida DiPace. *John F. Kennedy and the New Frontier.* New York, NY: Hill & Wang, 1966.

Fairlie, Henry. *The Kennedy Promise: The Politics of Expectation.* Garden City, NY: Doubleday, 1973.

Fay, Paul Burgess. *The Pleasure of His Company.* New York, NY: Harper & Row, 1966.

Firestone, Bernard J. *The Quest for Nuclear Stability: John F. Kennedy and the Soviet Union.* New York, NY: Greenwood Press, 1982.

Fuller, Helen. *Year of Trial: Kennedy's Crucial Decisions.* New York, NY: Harcourt, Brace & World, 1962.

Garrison, Jim. *On the Trail of the Assassins: My Investigation and Prosecution of the Murder of President Kennedy.* New York, NY: Sheridan Square Press, 1988.

Gromyko, Anatolii Andreevich. *Through Russian Eyes: President Kennedy's 1036 Days.* Washington, DC: International Library, 1973.

Harper, Paul, and Joanne P. Krieg, Editors. *John F. Kennedy: The Promise Revisited.* New York, NY: Greenwood Press, 1988.

Kunhardt, Philip B. *Life in Camelot.* Boston: Little, Brown & Co., 1989.

Lane, Mark. *Rush to Judgment.* New York, NY: Holt, Rinehart & Winston, 1966.

Lasky, Victor. *JFK: The Man and the Myth.* New York, NY: Macmillan, 1963.

Lincoln, Evelyn. *My Twelve Years with John F. Kennedy.* New York, NY: D. McKay Company, 1965.

Mailer, Norman. *The Presidential Papers.* New York, NY: Putnam, 1963.

Manchester, William Raymond. *The Death of a President: November 20 - November 25, 1963.* New York, NY: Harper & Row, 1967.

Manchester, William Raymond. *Portrait of a President: John F. Kennedy in Profile.* Boston: Little, Brown & Co., 1967.

Manchester, William Raymond. *One Brief Shining Moment: Remembering Kennedy.* Boston: Little, Brown & Co., 1988.

Martin, Ralph G. *A Hero for Our Time: An Intimate Story of the Kennedy Years.* New York, NY: Macmillan, 1983.

Meyers, Joan Simpson. *John F. Kennedy: As We Remember Him.* New York, NY: Atheneum, 1965.

Newman, John M. *JFK and Vietnam: Deception, Intrigue and the Struggle for Power.* New York, NY: Warner Books, 1992.

O'Donnell, Kenneth P., and David Powers. *Johnny, We Hardly Knew Ye: Memories of John Fitzgerald Kennedy.* Boston: Little, Brown & Co., 1983.

Paper, Lewis J. *John F. Kennedy: The Promise and the Performance.* New York, NY: Da Capo Press, 1980.

Parmet, Herbert S. *JFK: The Presidency of John F. Kennedy.* New York, NY: Dial Press, 1983.

Randall, Marta. *John F. Kennedy.* New York, NY: Chelsea House, 1988.

Rust, William J. *Kennedy in Vietnam.* New York, NY: Scribner, 1985.

Salinger, Pierre. *With Kennedy.* Garden City, NY: Doubleday, 1966.

Salinger, Pierre, and Sander Vanocur, Editors. *A Tribute to John F. Kennedy.* Chicago: Encyclopedia Brittanica, 1964.

Schlesinger, Arthur Meier. *A Thousand Days: John F. Kennedy in the White House.* Boston: Houghton Mifflin, 1965.

Sidey, Hugh. *John F. Kennedy, President.* New York, NY: Atheneum, 1964.

Sorensen, Theodore C. *Kennedy.* New York: Harper Collins, 1988.

Sorensen, Theodore C. *The Kennedy Legacy.* New York, NY: Macmillan, 1969.

Stone, Ralph A., Editor. *John F. Kennedy, 1917-1963.* Dobbs Ferry, NY: Oceana Publications, 1971.

Stoughton, Cecil, and Chester V. Clifton. *The Memories: JFK 1961-1963.* New York, NY: Norton, 1980.

Thompson, Robert Smith. *The Missiles of October: The Declassified Story of John F. Kennedy and the Cuban Missile Crisis.* New York, NY: Simon & Schuster, 1992.

Warren Commission. *The Official Warren Commission Report on the Assassination of President John F. Kennedy.* Washington, DC: U.S. Government Printing Office, 1964.

White, Theodore Harold. *The Making of the President, 1960.* New York, NY: Atheneum, 1961.

Wicker, Tom. *Kennedy Without Tears: The Man Behind the Myth.* New York, NY: Morrow, 1964.

Wofford, Harris. *Of Kennedys and Kings: Making Sense of the Sixties.* New York, NY: Farrar, Straus, Giroux, 1980.

YOUNG ADULT BIBLIOGRAPHY

Denenberg, Barry. *John Fitzgerald Kennedy: America's 35th President.* New York, NY: Scholastic Inc., 1988.

Falkof, Lucille. *John F. Kennedy: 35th President of the United States.* Ada, OK: Garrett Educational Corp., 1988.

Frolick, S.J. *Once There Was A President.* New York, NY: Black Star Publishing Co., 1980.

Graves, Charles P. *John F. Kennedy.* New York, NY: Dell Publishing Co., 1981.

Hoare, Stephen. *The Assassination of John F. Kennedy.* North Pomfret, VT: Trafalgar Square, 1989.

John F. Kennedy: Mini Play. Stockton, CA: Stevens & Shea, 1977.

Levine, I.E. *John Kennedy: Young Man in the White House.* Lakeville, CT: Grey Castle Press, 1991.

Mills, Judie. *John F. Kennedy.* New York, NY: Watts, 1988.

Index

Coming Soon From Excellent Books

Abraham Lincoln: Word For Word

The Dred Scott Speech

Now I protest against the counterfeit logic which concludes that, because I do not want a black woman for a slave I must necessarily want her for a wife. I need not have her for either, I can just leave her alone.

The Gettysburg Address

That these dead shall not have died in vain; that this nation, under God, shall have a new birth of freedom; and that government of the people, by the people, for the people, shall not perish from the earth.

The Emancipation Proclamation

That on the first day of January in the year of our Lord 1863, all persons held as slaves within any State whereof shall then be in rebellion against the United States, shall be then, thenceforward, and forever free.

The Second Inaugural Address

With malice toward none; with charity for all; with firmness in the right, as God gives us to see the right, let us strive on to finish the work we are in; to bind up the nation's wounds; to care for him who shall have borne the battle, and for his widow, and his orphan - to do all which may achieve and cherish a just and lasting peace, among ourselves, and with all nations.

ABRAHAM LINCOLN: WORD FOR WORD

EXCELLENT BOOKS ORDER FORM

(Please xerox this form so it will be available to other readers.)

Please send

_____ copy(ies) of JOHN F. KENNEDY: WORD FOR WORD
_____ copy(ies) of THOMAS JEFFERSON: WORD FOR WORD
_____ copy(ies) of ABORTION DECISIONS: THE 1970's
_____ copy(ies) of ABORTION DECISIONS: THE 1980's
_____ copy(ies) of ABORTION DECISIONS: THE 1990's
_____ copy(ies) of LANDMARK DECISIONS
_____ copy(ies) of LANDMARK DECISIONS II
_____ copy(ies) of LANDMARK DECISIONS III
_____ copy(ies) of THE ADA HANDBOOK

Name:_____**WITHDRAWN**_____

Address:_____

City:_____ State: _____ Zip: _____

Price: $19.95 for JOHN F. KENNEDY: WORD FOR WORD
$19.95 for THOMAS JEFFERSON: WORD FOR WORD
$15.95 for ABORTION DECISIONS: THE 1970's
$15.95 for ABORTION DECISIONS: THE 1980's
$15.95 for ABORTION DECISIONS: THE 1990's
$14.95 for LANDMARK DECISIONS
$15.95 for LANDMARK DECISIONS II
$15.95 for LANDMARK DECISIONS III
$15.95 for THE ADA HANDBOOK

Add $1 per book for shipping and handling
California residents add sales tax

OUR GUARANTEE: Any Excellent Book may be returned at any time for any reason and a full refund will be made.

Mail your check or money order to: Excellent Books, Post Office Box 927105, La Jolla, California 92192-7105
or call (619) 457-4895